FEAR-FREE FUNDRAISING:
HOW TO ASK
PEOPLE FOR MONEY

BY HOLLY MILLION

ISBN 1-4196-3495-X

This book is dedicated to my husband, Chris Million.

Thanks for your support, and

Thanks for the name.

And also to

Bill Geller and Leonard Ely, Jr.

Thanks for taking me on my first

donor solicitation meeting.

TABLE
OF
CONTENTS

INTRODUCTION

YOU need to raise money from individual donors. But, where to begin?

An individual giving program is often the last part of a nonprofit's fundraising program to develop, and yet, it's possibly the most important part of the program. Foundations are fickle. They stop funding after a few years of support, or, if their investment portfolios shrink in value, they suddenly stop accepting grant proposals. Government grants appear or disappear based on legislative whims and budgetary fiat. Corporate giving evaporates at the first sign of economic downturn. However, you can count on individual donors to give and give again, no matter what else is going on in the world.

But, how do you go about setting up an individual giving program if you don't have one already? How about your board of directors? Your board members are key players on your fundraising team. Are they pulling their weight? Or are they too afraid to fundraise? How can you make your fundraising events serve the goals of your individual giving plan? How do you set an annual goal and what are the steps you must take to get there?

The purpose of this book is to take the mystery and fear out of raising money from individual donors. The goal of this book is to give you the confidence you need to ask people for money—to turn you into a fearless fundraiser. If you or your board of directors have any apprehension about approaching individuals for contributions, this book will help you 1) visualize the steps to follow in introducing people to your organization, 2) actually take those steps, and 3) get people to write checks!

I have 15 years' experience as a fundraising professional, and I've worked for national nonprofits raising millions of dollars. I have worked with boards both green and seasoned. And, I have served on two nonprofit boards myself. I know the ins and outs of individual fundraising from both the staff and the board side. In addition to presenting basic fundraising concepts, each chapter of this book includes anecdotes from my personal fundraising experience to illustrate what works and what doesn't.

I'm writing this book because I didn't learn how to fundraise from an academic course, or from a workshop, or by learning from a mentor. I learned how to fundraise the hard way—by doing it. I'd like to share what I've learned with other nonprofit professionals and board members like you so you can get started faster and have more success sooner. There is no need to be afraid of individual donor fundraising—it's not rocket science, but, rather, common sense. If I can do it, so can you.

This book explores the complete process of individual giving including the following topics:

- Identifying your potential donors
- How to manage the individual giving process
- What role direct mail plays in the overall process
- How you can use house parties in your program
- How to make donors feel connected to your organization

- How to prepare for and set up face-to-face meetings to ask for money
- What to do if the potential donor says no
- What happens after the donor meeting

Read the book. Enjoy the anecdotes. Practice asking. Go out and ask. Yes, you, too, can be a fundraising superhero!

Holly Million
San Francisco, CA

FUNDRAISING OVERVIEW

YOU don't know me, but I already know something about your nonprofit organization. Your organization needs to create an individual giving program. Or, if your organization already has this type of program, it needs to enhance it significantly. Am I right? Well, that was easy. Most nonprofits start off in exactly the place you are in right now. The question you probably have is what does a successful individual giving program look like anyway? You have come to the right place to find out.

What does your fundraising program look like?

Chances are good that, if your organization is relatively young and understaffed, you have income coming from foundations, maybe a government grant or two, possibly a small event, and maybe a small, dedicated group of donors that might include the members of your board. An ideal funding program would have income coming from private foundations, smaller family foundations, local and Federal government grants, corporate foundations and corporate sponsorships, and small individual gifts and large individual gifts. The super-deluxe nonprofit funding program would also have a source of earned income (such as ticket sales, program fees, products, etc.), planned giving (where donors include your organization in their estate planning), rebate programs (such as eScrip), event income, and investment income.

Up to now, you probably haven't had time to think about developing an individual giving program. However, if you are reading this book, your organization has probably also reached the point where, if you don't start diversifying your income sources, particularly by getting more income from individuals, you're going to cease to grow, or even fail to maintain your current levels of program activity. Maybe that's already started to happen. Perhaps as your organization has grown beyond start-up status, you've lost a foundation funder—or two. You may be feeling the pinch of a shrinking economy. If your organization is a mid-sized organization that does not receive at least 50% of its income from individual giving, then you need to focus more of your attention on developing your individual-giving program. Eventually—probably sooner rather than later—those sources of foundation, government, and corporate gifts are going to run dry. Or at least go on vacation. You don't want to wait for that to happen. You want to take action now. As in today. Hey, what are you doing right now?

Your organization's funding streams will be unique depending on your programs and your field of service. For example, social service organizations often receive more money from government sources than other types of organizations. Also, large arts organizations often receive higher amounts of money from corporations because of their ability to offer these donors visibility and public recognition. However, whatever field your organization is in, whoever the clients served, whatever your mission, you could probably stand to raise more money from individuals. Like hot apple pie, it's just plain good!

What kinds of systems and tools do you need to do individual fundraising?

To have the best success with individual donor fundraising, I recommend having the following eight components in your program. If you are a younger or smaller organization, you may not have the resources to do all of these things. You can add pieces incrementally. It's not so important to have them created all at once as it is to keep working to build depth and complexity into your overall program.

1) A well-articulated fundraising plan

You need to start off each year with a written plan describing the actions you will take to raise money from all of the different sources you plan to ask for support. The plan needs to set dollar amounts to ask for and estimated dollar amounts for how much you anticipate receiving. You also need to determine when specific steps will take place, using a calendar to map them, and determine whether board or staff will take each action. Your goals can be set by benchmarking against last year's actual numbers. How many foundations did you approach? Which ones approved grants and when? Do you expect them to give again this year if you submit a proposal? What about individual donors? Without a written plan, you will be like a rudderless ship. If you're not careful, you'll end up crashing on the shoals of random funder whim! With a written plan, you can focus your actions to get the best results or thoughtfully diverge from the plan if your needs change or new opportunities arise.

2) An active, willing board of directors and leadership from your staff

If you are the development staff person for your organization, then you are going to play a pivotal role in what takes place. You need to be part salesperson, part cheerleader, part CEO, part quarterback, and part detective. Without you articulating the goals, describing the steps, expressing confidence in the plan, and partnering actively with the board, your organization cannot produce results. Sure, there are plenty of things you can do on your own, but, to be effective, you cannot solicit major donors by yourself. You may be tempted to go solo if your board is less than willing to join you on meetings with donor prospects. But, without a board that is gung-ho—or at least willing to pretend to be gung-ho—about going face to face with donor prospects, you simply will not meet your goals. If you are a board member, you need to take responsibility for your part in the individual donor process. There is no other part of the fundraising program that relies so much on board involvement. Open your address book, give your staff names to work with, and be an ambassador for the organization you care about so passionately.

3) A database of individual donor prospects

You need to organize the names and contact information of all the prospects you want to approach for support. Somehow, you have to be able to remember who has given what and when, what they like most about your programs, which events they have attended, what pieces of mail you want to send to them, and when they are due to have a face-to-face meeting. Make sure your database is in top shape. That means you have to standardize how you are entering data—abbreviate the same way every time; capitalize the same words every time; watch out for errors. Also, make sure you can sort data and make the kinds of reports you will need to analyze how you are doing so you can continually make better plans.

4) Research about the prospects to determine who has the best chance to give the most money

The simplest research you can do to find out more about individual donors is to meet one on one with your board members and ask them to tell you about their donor prospects. Ask them about the donors' quirks, pet peeves, passions—and neuroses (yes, most all have them). Ask the board member what other kinds of gifts this prospect makes that they are aware of. Take copious notes. Start a file for any donor prospects who have the capacity to give a major gift and put your hand-written notes in there so you can retrieve them later. Type any pertinent information directly into that donor prospect's entry in your database. You can also do a more systematic and in-depth kind of research on your prospects by using Internet and library tools. We will go into more depth about how to set up this kind of donor research program in Chapter Three.

5) Tools to communicate with prospects about your organization

Are you going to send your prospects information about your organization? Once per year? Multiple times per year? What kind of stuff? Many organizations use a newsletter, sent two or three times per year. Will you send invitations to events? How about direct mail to request your prospects' support? Start by taking an inventory of the materials you have that describe or represent your organization's work. For example, most organizations have stationery, envelopes, and business cards with some kind of logo and set typography. What about a brochure that describes what you do in a succinct and portable format? Outline what you have to work with and plan to create what you don't have but what will enhance your ability to communicate with these individuals. For more information about direct mail, see Chapter Five.

6) An annual campaign with a specific goal for how much to raise from individual donations

As part of your development plan, you will have a goal for how much money you plan to raise from individual donors. Once you know this number and once you know by when you need to raise it, you have the basis for a campaign. A campaign works. It makes what you're trying to do clear. It makes it concrete. "To build the new shelter/expand our core program/complete the website, our organization needs to raise $500,000 by December 31 of this year." Donors know how long they have to act, and they know what they're helping accomplish. You can also give your campaign a greater sense of urgency by setting a timeframe for raising the goal that is shorter rather than longer. Every time you communicate with your prospective donors, you want to talk to them about the campaign, and how their support will make a difference. When you print communication tools for your organization, you want to mention the campaign. As a board member, you want to understand the campaign and be able to speak as fluently about it as your staff members.

7) A lead gift that gives you the leverage to raise more gifts quickly

A lead gift is a gift that one donor makes to encourage others to give. Frequently, a lead gift is what is called a "challenge gift." That is, it is contingent upon the organization's raising an amount of money equivalent to what the challenge

HOT TIP

A LEAD GIFT
HELPS YOU
RAISE MORE
MONEY, FASTER

donor is giving. Sometimes, the gift is contingent upon your raising two times the gift amount, or even three or more times. Oftentimes, the donor will be someone whose name will carry weight with the other donors to your organization. Or, perhaps the individual who makes this kind of gift will prefer to remain anonymous.

Lead gifts are powerful. They help you raise money faster and in greater quantities. Donors tend to be cautious people. They like to know what others are thinking and doing. If someone prominent comes forward to make a very large gift to your organization, then your other donors feel reassured. If the gift is a challenge gift, they may feel some excitement knowing that their gift is doubled in value due to the match provided by the challenge. And, if there is a deadline for making the match, they will feel some urgency and ideally act to make a gift sooner rather than later. Challenge gifts are powerful stuff. Do everything you can, every time you can, to secure one of these babies!

8) Ways to keep donors connected with your organization on an ongoing basis

Once someone has made a gift to your organization, don't

take him or her for granted. You need to thank donors, and thanking them more than once for a single gift is not going to hurt. As donors display loyalty, and possibly even a growing commitment to your organization, find ways to get them even more

HOT TIP

RELATIONSHIP IS THE KEY TO INDIVIDUAL DONOR FUNDRAISING

involved in your work. Key donors can be recruited to serve on your committees, including the fundraising committee. Your biggest major donors should be prospects for your board of directors. The main reason to get people more closely tied to what you do is that the closer they get, the more they will want to keep giving money, and more of it.

As your individual donor program grows, continue to refine the mechanisms you have in place to connect with donors and help them feel connected to you.

A maximized fundraising program squeezes every ounce of potential income from every source. No foundation is left unturned. No individual donor gathers moss. It is unlikely that your fundraising program will ever be fully maximized, but it is something good to aim for. The higher you aim, the more money you will raise.

Now that we have reviewed the major pieces of a complete individual giving program, let's take a more in-depth look at how individual giving works.

What role does individual giving play?

The key to individual giving is relationships. You'll hear this mantra repeated throughout this book. Individual giving is all about relationships. The reason is that good individual fundraising cannot exist without real understanding of the people who are giving, their personalities, their interests, and their minds and hearts. Once you understand and wholeheartedly embrace this idea, the world of individual fundraising will open up to you. Because individual donors connect to the organizations they give to in a very personal and often very emotional way, your organization can come to count on these donors' passion for your work. They will develop a dedication to giving, an emotional impetus for giving you money. They will come to give regularly, perhaps increasing their giving over time. And, when the going gets tough, perhaps because some crisis hits your organization, they will rally to your side. If a tornado touches down and destroys your facility, they will open their checkbooks and help pay for a new building. If the economy heads into recession, they will continue to give and possibly increase their giving because they know your work is so important—maybe even more so during a bad economy. Government funding will shrivel and die. Foundation boards will go into hiding, meeting for three years to rewrite their guidelines rather than accept any new proposals. Corporate philanthropists will head for the hills. But your individual donors will keep on giving.

Because individual giving programs are built upon hundreds, if not thousands, of individuals' contributions, whether one person or several people don't give one year has less impact than if one foundation or several stop sending you grant checks. The thousands of checks from these donors are like thousands of bricks in a wall. If one brick crumbles, the wall still stands. Your organization must have that kind of stability.

Individual giving is also important because each person who gives to your organization represents an entire network of people—all the people that the individual donor knows, works with, is related to, shops with, goes to school with. Individual donors can tell their friends about you, and that makes it easier for your organization to become known and to attract more gifts.

Why do individuals choose to give to nonprofit organizations?

Isn't it wonderful that we have such a thing as nonprofit

organizations that perform so many wonderful services in our communities? So many beautiful performing arts events! So many human needs met! So many streams protected, forests preserved, and parklands cleaned up! And yet, none of this would be possible without monetary contributions. Our economic system recognizes charitable contributions to nonprofit organizations as a tax-deductible activity, and that is a big motivation for many people who give. They can write the gift off of their taxes. But, for most people, a tax write-off isn't a good enough reason to give. They want to know that their gift is "making a difference." Almost everyone is motivated on some level by wanting the world to be a better place, and nonprofit organizations provide a visible and convenient way to fulfill that desire. If someone has a particular cause that is near to his or her heart, a particular interest, disability, disease, or affiliation, chances are good that there is also a nonprofit organization out there working to serve that interest, disability, etc. There's a veritable Vegas-style buffet of nonprofits to give to.

HOT TIP

PEOPLE ARE MORE LIKELY TO DONATE TO CAUSES AND ORGANIZATIONS THAT THEIR FRIENDS SUPPORT

There is another reason, however, that people give to nonprofits. And it's probably the most overlooked reason of all. People give because someone asks them. People who aren't asked tend not to give. People who are asked do. It's simple and true. Moreover, if these people are asked to give by someone they know, someone who is close to them or connected to them in some way, they are even more likely to give. They think, "If George is asking me to give to this organization, then it must be pretty darn good, since George is such a darn good guy." Furthermore, if the person asking is a really close friend, they are likely to give a more substantial gift, and to continue giving over a longer period of time. They believe that George knows what he's talking about and believe that this must be a great organization—also, they don't want to disappoint George.

How does hearing a story impact a donor's decision to give?

One of the keys to individual donor fundraising is being able to tell a human story that resonates in the heart of the donor. The nonprofit organizations that succeed best at this type of fundraising are the ones that find a way to put a human face on their story. For some organizations, such as the ones that serve children or women or homeless individuals, this job is much easier, because they serve human beings.

For other types of organizations, such as environmental organizations, for example, it's a little harder, because their missions might be a little more abstract, a little less connected to serving individuals. Nonetheless, they have to find a way to tell a story that an individual donor can connect with, or personally identify with. If you don't have a human face to put on your story, how about a furry little animal face? A baby bird? Pandas? Where do I send my check?

HOT TIP

IF IT INVOLVES
A PANDA,
PEOPLE WILL
WRITE A CHECK

Are big gifts more important than small gifts?

You might think that large gifts from very wealthy people are the most important kind of gift to focus on. You might think that small gifts might be more important because it's easier for people to write small checks and keep writing them. Actually, you need gifts of all sizes to have a healthy individual giving program. You don't want one type of gift at the exclusion of other types of gifts—that's right, you want all the gifts!

The important question here is how do we define large and small? The fact is, these are not precise terms. In fact, a "major" gift (i.e., a "large" gift) is a term that you are going to apply as you see fit to your pool of donors. What one organization considers a major gift may be small potatoes to a different organization. What is important is to select a size of gift that defines a level of service that you will provide to the giver of that gift. Perhaps the amount is $500. That means that you will give people who are able to give $500 or more a higher degree of attention and more personalized service so that they will feel connected to your organization and be willing to continue to write checks of this size or greater. Does that mean you take for granted donors who give less than this or treat them with less respect? No, of course not! But you don't spend as much time on each one of them. You don't have that much time or that many resources. You have to make a decision about how to allocate your resources to get the best return for your organization.

HOT TIP

BIG GIFTS
AND SMALL
GIFTS WORK
IN SYNERGY

There is a special synergy that happens between large gifts and small gifts. Major donors act as leaders within your donor pool. Their willingness to give a large gift and to let you recognize them for giving it can help you attract more small gifts. Donors of smaller gifts are often impressed to see that some local philanthropists, some of whom may be well known around town for their giving, have chosen to make a substantial gift to your organization. Likewise, your donors who make a substantial gift may be more inclined to do this if you can demonstrate to them that you work hard for every possible gift and that you have built a "base" that will support the organization's work. Also, major donors who give a special lead gift or challenge gift are directly communicating with donors at every other level, basically inviting them to participate in a group process to meet a financial goal on behalf of the organization. Achieving these kinds of goals would not be possible without donors great and small.

It's also important to realize that, while donors may start off making a small gift, over time they may increase their giving. Major donors will emerge from the ranks of the smaller donors. Your job is to coax those potential major donors to come forward. In any case, you want to encourage all of your donors to increase their giving levels and the frequency at which they are contributing.

The following chart shows the basic shape your individual giving program needs to take to have this healthy balance between large (and medium) and small gifts.

THE DONOR PYRAMID

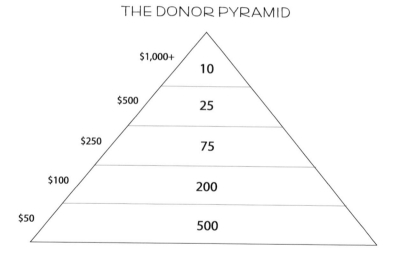

What is the role of staff in fundraising?

Staff have a vested interest in running a successful individual giving program. The reason is that their livelihoods depend upon bringing money into the organization and keeping their paychecks coming. Staff work full time managing fundraising for the organization. Because of this, they need to be the people who take the lead on individual fundraising.

Staff, usually a director of development, sometimes the executive director, provides the leadership needed to run the program. The director of development is often the quarterback, calling plays in the huddle, snapping the ball, and throwing passes to board members. The director of development writes the development plan for the organization for the board's approval. The director of development or other staff manage the prospects provided by the board, tracking who has given, how much and when. The staff person oversees all of the cultivation taking place for the organization and provides assistance for board members who need help getting packets to prospects in the mail or who need a financial report to show a donor. It is also the staff person who plays an indispensable role in the actual face-to-face solicitation meetings with donors. Because it is the staff person who actually asks for a gift of a specific amount.

HOT TIP

THE DIRECTOR OF DEVELOPMENT IS LIKE A QUARTERBACK, THROWING THE BALL; BOARD MEMBERS RUN WITH AND CATCH THE BALL—THEY SCORE TOUCHDOWNS

What is the role of board in fundraising?

Board members also play an indispensable role in fundraising. They provide the main introductions for new people to the organization and its work. Without the board members' willingness to make these kinds of introductions, there is no individual giving program.

Board members take a lead with their own donor prospects and engage in regular cultivation efforts. If the organization is hosting an event for potential donors, it is the board members' responsibility to call up their friends and encourage them to come. It is also the board members' responsibility to call their friends to set up the face-to-face solicitation meeting that the board member and staff member will attend together with the prospect. Lastly, in the solicitation meeting, it is the board member's responsibility to make the prospective donor feel comfortable and at ease. It is his or her job to talk enthusiastically and energetically about the organization and why it is worthwhile from a personal standpoint.

What happens when board and staff work on their own versus together?

Oftentimes, board members go off and do their own individual fundraising. Or, a nonprofit staff person will try to do a solicitation meeting alone, working from the prospect lists he researched or got from the board of directors. Unfortunately, both of these solo efforts are likely doomed to failure. Certainly, some money might be raised, but it will probably be much less than would have been raised had the two team members worked together. Even more likely, the

TROPHY CASE

I once had a reluctant board member who had gotten burned by a solicitation meeting gone wrong (because she tried to do it alone). Subsequently, she was afraid to ask anyone for money. Little did she know, a friend of hers on the prospect list she'd given me was a donor I'd successfully solicited for another organization. Working off the script, I called the prospect myself to ask if he wanted to have lunch with me and his friend. He said yes. Was she surprised when I called to tell her John had agreed to a solicitation meeting! When we came back with $5,000, her confidence for solicitation revived.

result will be no money raised, because the solo players cannot pull off the successful donor ask alone—this ask requires a combination of personal connection and personal detachment that calls for a duo. Find a way to get both board and staff players to work together.

The never-ending job of board development

In order to succeed—in fact, in order to survive—your organization must constantly be engaged in the process of board development. As a staff person, you have to identify potential board members, from your donor pool, from your volunteers, or from the community at large, and recruit them to the board at all times. As a board member, you need to think about how you will replace yourself when it's your time to step off the board. Who among your friends or colleagues would make the same kind of conscientious, dedicated board member that you are?

In either case, staff and board must be honest with poten-

HOT TIP

YOU MUST
ALWAYS BE
DEVELOPING
YOUR BOARD
IN ORDER TO
SUCCEED WITH
INDIVIDUAL
DONOR
FUNDRAISING

tial board members about the role board members will play in individual donor fundraising. It doesn't pay to hide from the prospective new member the fact that everyone on the board will be included in fundraising. You don't want him or her to join the board and then spring the news that friends must be cultivated for gifts! And yet, this is what so many organizations do. Don't do it. Be up front about fundraising.

Also, if you look for potential new board members from among your largest donors, you make your work that much easier. These people already understand and accept that your organization needs to raise money!

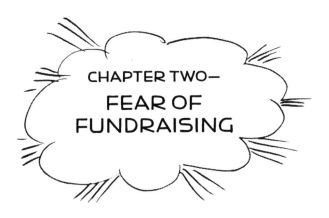

CHAPTER TWO—
FEAR OF FUNDRAISING

B Y NOW, we've all heard about the famous study in which the test subjects ranked their fear of public-speaking above their fear of dying. Of course, that study didn't ask these same people how they felt about asking someone for money. That's too bad, because I'm sure if they'd been asked they would have ranked asking for money well above both public-speaking and death as something that gives them a chill. Most normal individuals are terrified about asking someone else for money. If you are not afraid to do this, there is probably something unusual about you. Either you're a dynamic salesperson, a seasoned development staff person, or you've been forced to ask for money enough times that you are sufficiently numbed to the task. Many people are ashamed to admit that they are afraid to do a donor solicitation. In fact, they are sane and reasonable individuals!

What are the reasons why people are afraid to ask for money?

People are afraid to ask other people for money for a couple of key reasons. First of all, although the United States is the preeminent capitalistic country in the world, somehow, money has gotten a bad name around here. As you know, we've got "Money is the root of all evil" and "filthy lucre" and "filthy rich" to overcome before we feel comfortable with money itself. Just as it's not polite to talk about sex or politics in a social setting, so is it considered gauche to bring up the subject of money. Going onward from there, we also come to another root cause of fundraising fear. And that fear is more personal. People are afraid that the people they ask for money—who in many cases will be people they know well, perhaps intimately, such as their relatives, friends, and colleagues—will get angry with them for asking. "If I ask my friend to make a contribution to the March of Quarters, he'll never speak to me again," is the prevailing thought. People are afraid that they'll have to deal with an immediate angry response or a more passive-aggressive response. The potential donor may not show any sign of offense face to face, but he or she might harbor a grudge. Even if the potential donor does not blow up, people are afraid that he or she will say no and that they will not know what to do when that happens.

HOT TIP

NORMAL PEOPLE ARE AFRAID TO ASK FOR MONEY

   Some of these fears may be well founded. It is possible— even likely—that the potential donor will say no. Count on potential donors saying no. We'll tell you how to handle that eventuality in Chapter Seven. For now, we are here to exorcise the causes of irrational fundraising fears. Maybe the person will become angry. But how often do people explode in rage in normal, everyday life? Perhaps the potential donor will not become visibly angry but will harbor a grudge. Maybe, but why? Life is short. Healthy people move on. No, people rarely get angry when you ask them for money to support a worthwhile cause that you believe in and maybe are even passionate about. They don't get angry when you invite them to participate in something that makes you excited and makes you feel good. No! In fact, they may be honored or flattered that you want to share the good feelings with them. You were looking for something to do that would make the world a better place, and so are other people. You are not the only good-hearted person in the world. And this is what you have to keep in mind

HOT TIP

SUCCESSFUL
FUNDRAISERS
GET OVER THEIR
FEAR OF ASKING
FOR MONEY

when irrational fears of angry, cold, bitter people creep into your thoughts of fundraising. Don't forget—fear is the enemy.

Your asking for a donation is an invitation you extend to the person you ask. It is an invitation to make his life bigger. To find meaning. To touch someone's life. To make the world a better place.

These are the things you are offering a potential donor by inviting him or her to support a cause you believe in. You don't think the cause is dirty or irrelevant. You think it's great. You think it's so great that you not only write checks to support it, but you spend your precious personal time showing up at events, eating rubber chicken lunches at the annual fundraiser, and sitting through board meetings. Or, you think it's so great that you gave up your lucrative career in sales and marketing for a major multinational widget manufacturer in order to slave long hours for low wages working full-time for this nonprofit. You are believable. Because you walk the talk and write the checks yourself. There must be something good here. Incredibly good. Your friends and colleagues will see that immediately. And they'll wonder why you are holding out on them. How come you haven't invited them to join in? Seriously? If you stop focusing so selfishly and self-consciously upon yourself and how you'll look when you ask for a gift, you will quickly get over it and get on with doing the fundraising that needs to happen.

Here is a very important secret. If you remember one thing from this book, remember this next idea: the main difference between organizations that succeed and those that fail is the ones that succeed have people involved who are willing to ask for money. If you ask for money, your organization can succeed and may even thrive. If you do not ask for money from individuals, then I can pretty much guarantee that your organization will eventually sputter and die out. Knowing this, why would you not muster the courage to ask individuals you know to give money for the sake of your organization?

HOT TIP

JUST LIKE YOU, OTHER PEOPLE WANT TO MAKE A DIFFERENCE IN THE WORLD AND FEEL GOOD ABOUT THEMSELVES

So what can you do to overcome your fear of fundraising? Remember these key points. First, remember that most fears about fundraising are unlikely to come true. Second, remember that the main reason you are asking is because you are supporting a great organization that does immeasurable (or even better, measurable) good in this world. Next, you can plan, cultivate, and learn from mistakes. We will get into more detail coming up next about what cultivation involves, but for now, it's enough to know that it is basically building a relationship between the potential donor and the organization. You don't jump in cold to asking somebody for a contribution before you have developed his interest in and his relationship with the organization. When it is time to ask, you will know, and then you can set up a solicitation meeting. Lastly, you can remember to practice asking by doing role-playing with your colleagues, board members, and volunteers to the organization. We have a big chapter on solicitation practice coming up later in the book. Last, and far from least, you can go out and make real requests of real people. There's nothing like the real thing—I dare you to try.

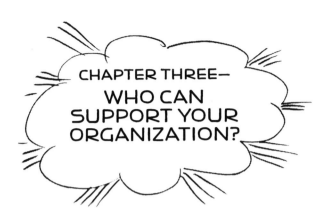

CHAPTER THREE—
WHO CAN SUPPORT YOUR ORGANIZATION?

THERE are several key groups of people you should look to for contributions to your organization. The first and most obvious group is your own board of directors. It is one of the primary duties of the board to be a solid, generous pool of donors to the organization. Surprisingly, too many organizations exist out in the world who don't expect their board members to give, and too many board members exist out in the world who don't think to write a check to the cause they claim to support. Your organization needs to aim for 100% board participation in gift-giving. By having your board's full financial commitment in a personal way, your organization signals to the whole world that it really and truly is worthy of support.The last thing you want to happen is for a major donor prospect to ask who gives and to be told that the list does not include all of your

HOT TIP

EVERY, SINGLE PERSON ON YOUR BOARD OF DIRECTORS NEEDS TO MAKE A PERSONALLY SIGNIFICANT CONTRIBUTION EACH AND EVERY YEAR

board members. If they don't give, why should she? Furthermore, each board member should make a gift that is "personally significant," that is, not some chump change, but rather a gift they can really feel to be a contribution. As they say, give 'til it hurts (or at least produces some sensation).

One of the simplest and best ways to make sure your board members all make an annual gift to your organization is first to tell prospective board members who are considering joining your board that this is a requirement for membership. Next, create a personal pledge form that each board member receives and fills out once a year that asks him or her how much the organization can expect as his or her contribution that year, as well as when the gift will be made. Last, in the first board meeting of the year, have your board chair announce that all board members are being asked to give a personally significant gift that year. If there are still any people who don't seem to get it after this many hints, have the chair of your development committee or another board member who is a peer to the lagging individual give a gentle, or not so gentle, reminder to pony up.

Once you've gotten your whole board to contribute, the next step in finding out who your prospective donors are is to ask yourself the following questions:

Who donates now?

The people who are your best prospects for future gifts are the people who have already given to your organization. By writing a check, giving a gift of stock, or attending a fundraising event, they have already demonstrated interest in your organization and a desire to support your work. Donors who have given are qualified prospects. That is, they have separated themselves out from the general pool of unqualified donors by showing their interest through giving money.

As donors give, track their gifts, and see if you notice trends, such as individuals who give every time you ask. Or, individuals who give more when you ask for more. Or, individuals who send a check and a note asking for more information. Any sign of interest is potentially a sign of a donor worth getting to know better.

TROPHY CASE

While working for a medical organization, I met with a new major donor in New York who asked if we had a medical fellowship program. I told her we didn't, but that I would bring her idea back to the office. Six months later, the organization hired a new medical director who told me one of his dreams was to start a fellowship program. I told him I knew the right donor for that program. We met with her to ask for $65,000 to launch the fellowship—which is now named after her grandfather. This is a great finish to a story of a donor whose first gift came through a direct mail appeal.

Who could give if you asked them?

Every organization possesses an invisible network. This network starts with the board of directors, extends outward to friends of the board members, then outward again to friends of the friends of the board members, and finally to the larger community. Your job is to reach out to people in all of these circles extending out from the board. The more actively you spread the word about the organization and its good work, the more you will inspire people to get involved, write a check, tell their friends. The table below shows how these circles are arranged. You'll notice that the key to making the whole thing come together is the board of directors. The board is the key to all individual donor fundraising. Without a strong, passionate, committed, and brave board of directors, individual donor fundraising just doesn't work. Your job if you are on the staff is to nurture and develop your board so you always have energized, fresh, willing board members. Your job if you are on a board is to fulfill this important role that nobody but you can perform for the organization. If you are too afraid, don't follow through, or don't work with staff, then your organization will suffer.

Your board members are the key people to introduce new prospective donors to your mission and programs. By providing your organization with names and contact information for people they know and are willing to introduce, your board members start the whole fundraising ball rolling. It starts with an action as simple as opening up their address books or thumbing through their rolodexes.

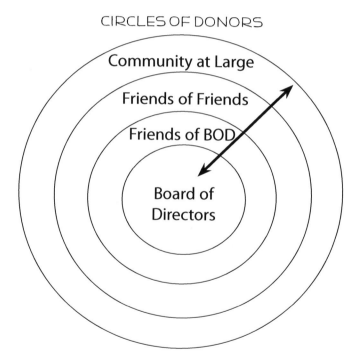

CIRCLES OF DONORS

Who exists in the community who could give if they knew you existed?

After you have done the most important steps listed above, then and only then, look at who gives to other, similar organizations that exist in the community. Get annual reports from these organizations, or look on their websites for names. Read the paper and see who is attending fundraising events for specific organizations. Find out the contact information for these people and put them on your mailing list. Make sure they get personal invitations to your fundraising events. Or call and ask if they would like to visit your facility in person to see what you do. Cultivate them.

What's the most effective way to gather names from your board?

At the end of this chapter is a prospective donor information form. Each year, if you're staff, you will want to give a copy of this form, or an electronic spreadsheet, to your board of directors so they can update their prospects and add new ones. If you're board, you want to be as generous as possible in supplying names and contact information. Have you provided ten names? Why not twenty? If you have provided twenty, can you dig deeper and give 50, 100, or more?

As an experiment, at your next board meeting, ask your board members to bring their address books and contact lists and write down the names and addresses of ten people they know that they could introduce to your organization and who could become donors. If you have already done this exercise recently with your organization, do it again right now, and see who your board members can think of that they haven't thought of before.

Once you have the list of new prospects, you can jumpstart cultivation by sending the new people a letter from their friend on your board. This introductory letter will notify the recipient that his friend is on the board of directors of your organization and will provide an introductory description of what your organization does. You can also include a remit envelope to get on the fast track for giving with people who will be impressed simply because of their friend's involvement.

The following are samples of different tools and templates to support your individual donor fundraising program. Use these to create tools tailored to your specific needs. The first sample is an individual fundraising program plan for a young, up-and-coming organization that was about to launch this part of its program. Notice how various components of a successful individual donor program are integrated to establish the regular contact needed to cultivate and solicit donors.

SAMPLE—INDIVIDUAL DONOR FUNDRAISING PLAN

ArtOrg Individual Donor Plan 2005

I. Plan Summary

This plan defines ArtOrg's individual donor plan for 2005, with an overview of the plan for 2006 through 2007. Ideally, the 2005 plan will be reviewed frequently during the year with adjustments made as necessary. The goal is to build a basic, functioning individual donor program that can grow over time. ArtOrg has a diversified revenue plan except for individual gifts. By developing this part of the fundraising program, ArtOrg will gain more financial stability and can take on new and bigger projects.

II. Individual Donor Program Components

A. Annual campaign

This year's campaign will take advantage of ArtOrg's upcoming 10th anniversary which officially happens in March 2006. The official title of the campaign will be "The ArtOrg 10th Anniversary Campaign." The purpose of the campaign will be to raise unrestricted program funds to celebrate and honor ArtOrg's achievements in its 10th anniversary year and to make ArtOrg stronger and ready to take on bigger challenges in the near future. The dollar goal for the campaign will be up to $30,000 with a challenge grant and as low as $15,000 without a challenge grant. The deadline for meeting the campaign goal will be December 31, 2005. This initial campaign will be conducted as one "year-long" campaign. In the future, you can divide the annual campaign into a spring segment and a fall segment, using separate lead/challenge gifts and having different themes for each segment.

B. Lead gift

The goal is to secure a lead gift of approximately $15,000. You will also be able to work with a lead gift of $10,000 or even $5,000 but no smaller. Depending on what size lead gift you can secure, you will frame the campaign accordingly. This gift can come from a foundation, individuals, or a combination of the two. The lead/challenge gift can also be created from several individuals' contributions.

Some potential sources for the lead gift are:

a) Memphis Foundation—Zoe will ask the program officer about the possibility of receiving a staff-designated challenge grant to kick off the individual giving program.

b) Bob and Becky Prime—current donors who may be able to contribute toward the lead gift

c) Rob's individual sources—Rob knows some individuals who might be able to contribute $3,000 to $5,000 toward the challenge.

d) Kristine Smith—she is a major donor and the sister of a staff member who may be open to providing a larger gift toward the challenge

e) Dr. Eugene and Carol Sheldon—current major donors

f) Landlord—he might be able to do a large gift toward the challenge; if not, he can contribute toward the campaign.

g) Two rich neighbors—the neighbors connected with Wal-Mart and Odwalla should be cultivated and asked for a large gift either as a lead gift or as support for the campaign.

h) Joe Carson—Rob has a contact with this local philanthropist who works for a law firm.

I) Jonathan Young's network—he may know some people for this purpose; in any case, he should be heavily involved in the campaign and can help build the mailing list.

j) Others?—identify any others we have not discussed.

C. Database management

This is the top priority. You need to gather all information and put it into an electronic format, preferably in a software program that will be easy to use and which will generate reliable reports in the future. Rob has friends in high-tech who could help set up a new database where all of the information on donors and prospects can be organized. You should recruit a team of dedicated and reliable volunteers to take on the initial data-entry project under Helen's supervision. This will allow this task to get done quickly for minimal cost. When this task is done, you should have a mailing list of a couple thousand people minimum.

Current pools of potential donors to add to the mailing list include:

1) Volunteers—approximately 1,000 per year; have 400 emails collected; have mechanism for gathering information from volunteers that can be made more effective.

2) Collective—there are 10 to 15 regular people involved with the clusters.

3) Donors—there is an existing list of 37 donors who can be segmented into regular and major donors; some of these individuals can also be asked to provide a list of additional people to put on the mailing list.

4) Renters—there are 400 people on this list.

5) Market—there are about 500 people whose contact information has been gathered by tabling at the market; tabling should continue regularly during the campaign.

6) Website—there are between 200 and 500 emails that have been collected through the listserv, although there was a loss of data last November when the service provider closed the site down.

7) Neighbors—there are some neighbors who have said they would like to get more involved; there are two rich neighbors who should be cultivated for a large gift; the landlord may also be willing to provide a list of names of people to put on mailing list.

8) Event attendees—there are 1,000s of people attending events at ArtOrg each year, including raves and Burning Man events; these people cannot be "poached" because they "belong" to other organizations, however, there should be a table/kiosk where they can sign up to be on the ArtOrg mailing list or where they can find out more about the campaign and contribute.

9) Studio members—these people may be willing to provide lists of names to add to the mailing list.

10) Vendors—they already currently give discounts on their services, but they might contribute cash, too, if they knew about a campaign.

11) Others?

D. Research on donors

Need to begin dividing donors into regular and major donor categories. For ArtOrg, a major gift can be defined as $250 or more. As your program grows, this number will go up. You want to create paper files where you maintain information about key major donors in addition to the electronic information you keep in the database. Over time, these files will grow. When you receive lists from different people to add to the mailing list, ask the person giving you the list if there is anyone on the list who could give a gift of $250 or more. Take notes about those major donor prospects, including what they already give to, how the person knows they have wealth, their likes and dislikes, etc.

Some key major donors or sources for major donors include:

1) Nickel Fund—at the Community Foundation of Santa Fe

2) Times Fund—individual donor

3) Helen's contacts—rich uncle, other rich people her parents know

4) Zoe's contacts—sister at Smith Barney

5) Rob's contacts—VP at Hair Club for Men, his parents, some contacts from the high-tech world

6) Tom Anderson—not a big donor himself, but able to make introductions

7) Chris Duncan—able to provide contacts

8) Current majors—the people listed above under the Lead Gift section are also major donors.

9) Others?

E. Tools

These are the devices you have to communicate with donors, build their relationship with ArtOrg, and ask them to contribute. You need to increase your use of some of these tools and create other tools from scratch.

1) Direct mail—ArtOrg just sent a letter that included brochure, DVD, postcard and reply envelope to list of 37 donors. Need to send two direct mail appeals each year, one in the spring and one in mid-November. This letter should go to the entire mailing list and include a reply device; need to get bulk mail permit if you don't already have one; keep cost of printing the letter low; give people the option to get off the mailing list if they want to.

2) Email—emails are now sent to a members list; it is basic, monthly, and sporadic. Can turn this into a device driving more people to the website; have embedded links that let people donate in response. You need to schedule email updates on the calendar so

they happen regularly and support your print-media outreach. You want to gather more emails from the main group of people who are already on the mailing list or who are about to be added to the mailing list.

3) House parties—house parties will become one of the most important parts of the ArtOrg individual donor program; for details on how house parties work, see the attached description; some potential house party hosts include Zoe, Jonathan Young, and Kristine Smith. This tool should be developed during this first year of the program and increase next year. Start recruiting new house party hosts early for 2006.

4) Website—need to re-do the design of the website, write new copy, make it more obvious how to donate to the organization, and improve the ability of the website to collect people's contact information. Rob has a designer friend who can work for $10 per hour doing this work.

5) Newsletter—A 2 to 4-page newsletter is possible; would suggest doing one 2x per year. Determine the least expensive way to print and mail this. You can seek pro bono or discount printing as one option.

6) Events—ArtOrg is going to hire an events coordinator, which will help with this further developing this source of income.

7) Other print materials— brochure, DVD of TV show, postcard and reply card.

8) Perks/benefits—tee-shirts, CD, other tangible items to give donors; Rob has a connection with two tee-shirt companies and may be able to help with free/cheap tee-shirts

9) Other?

F. Board development

The future of the individual donor program depends upon having a strong, vibrant board that includes people who 1) have money, 2) know people with money, and 3) are willing and able to ask other people for money. Need to recruit more people to join the board, making it clear to them up front that fundraising will play a very key role in the future. Need to be careful about whom to add to the board because of the collective structure of the organization. You want to include people who can fundraise but who understand and support the mission and vision of ArtOrg. You should keep an ongoing roster of candidates as names surface.

Some potential board members include:

1) Matt Gomez

2) Chris Coltraine

3) William and Johanna Nunez

4) Real estate expert

5) Lawyer

6) Architect

7) Helen's family friend—who works for the Italian Center may know of some candidates

8) Others?

III. Timeline/To Do List

2005

The top priorities for 2005 are 1) getting data management under control and 2) putting in place most of the basic components of the individual donor plan, including securing a lead/challenge gift and running a successful campaign.

April

- Contact Rob's connection to come in to redesign the data management system, including a system for designating which people get what kinds of mailings and communications.

- Get Rob's contacts to overhaul the ArtOrg website.

- Rob help write new content for the website.

- Helen gather all information from every ArtOrg sub-group, including name, address, phone, emails—whatever is available should be brought into one physical location in preparation for data-entry project.

- Apply for nonprofit bulk mail permit if you don't already have one.

- Set dates for house parties with Zoe, Jonathan, and Kristine and have them create a guest list they give to you for the general mailing list.

May

- Set up meetings with all key donors to discuss the annual giving campaign and ask if they can help contribute a portion of the lead gift; if you have already secured the lead gift by the time you meet with certain donors, then meet to ask them for a contribution in response to the challenge.

- Zoe approach program officer at Memphis Fdn. about potential for lead/challenge gift.

- Recruit volunteers to help Helen enter all data in the new database.

- Review regular data collection processes and see where they can be improved; this includes how you collect contact information from volunteers and event attendees, how you table and sign people up, how the website collects data, etc.

- Create a simple form people can fill in with contact information for their potential donors—give this form to the board, Tom, Chris, neighbors, other key people who can provide more names and addresses. Add their names to Helen's collection of data.

- Meet with any major donors you didn't meet already.

- Host brainstorming meeting with key people to identify new potential recruits for the board of directors.

- Have volunteers enter data.

- Determine if you will have a challenge gift or not.

- Set goal, focus, and deadline for the annual campaign—amount will change based on whether or not a lead gift is secured

June

- Finish set-up of database architecture.

- Make sure the following are in the database and included in communications/direct asks for gifts:

Nickel Fund at the Community Foundation of Santa Fe

Times Fund individual donor

Helen's contacts—rich uncle, other rich people her parents know

Zoe's contacts—sister at Smith Barney

Rob's contacts—VP at Hair Club for Men, his parents, some contacts from the high-tech world

- Send invitations for first house party
- Meet with any more major donors you didn't meet already.
- Make giant "thermometer" to track progress toward the campaign goal and update it as contributions come in.
- Contact potential new board members.
- Volunteers finish entering data.
- Once you know the campaign goal, send email to entire list to announce the campaign and include a link to your website for immediate donations.
- First house party toward end of June.

July

- Send invitations for second house party.
- Seek donation of tee-shirts or other goods to offer as donation premiums.
- Recruit volunteers to table at all events, including market, to gather names and contributions.
- Contact potential new board members.
- Review individual donor plan and make adjustments.
- Enter new data in database.
- Second house party toward end of July.

August

- Send invitations for third house party

- Send email to entire list to update the campaign with link to website for donations.

- Contact potential new board members.

- Enter new data in database.

- Design two-page newsletter with remit envelope inside.

- Print newsletter.

- Review individual donor plan and make adjustments.

- Prepare mailing information from database.

- Third house party toward end of August.

September

- Enter new data in database.

- Send email to main list to update the campaign with link to website for donations.

- Mail first ArtOrg newsletter with remit envelope inside.

October

- Write draft year-end appeal letter.

- Enter new data in database.

- Review individual donor plan and make adjustments.

- Design year-end appeal letter and complete layout.

- Prepare mailing information from database.

November

- Ask all of your board members to make a personal contribution by the end of December to help ArtOrg reach the individual campaign goal.

- Enter new data in database.

- Print direct mail and assemble for mailing.

- Send email to main list to update the campaign with link to website for donations.

- Review individual donor plan and make adjustments.
- Mail first year-end appeal letter before Thanksgiving.

December

- Send email to main list to update the campaign with link to website for donations.
- Do year-end visits and phonecalls with key donors to ask them for contributions to complete the campaign goal.
- At end of month, send email announcing the successful completion of the goal.

2006

The top priorities for 2006 are 1) developing the board so that it includes people with key skills, such as lawyers, real estate experts, and architects, but most importantly, people who can and will help raise money, and 2) doing a full annual donor campaign from the beginning of the year.

Key additions will be:

— Increasing the dollar amount of the annual campaign.

— Dividing the campaign into a spring component and a fall component, each ideally with its own challenge gift.

— Securing donor prospects from all new board members and beginning to cultivate them.

— Doing a spring appeal letter and a fall appeal letter.

— Sending two newsletters, one in January, one in September.

— Developing a set of donor "tiers" and benefits that helps segment the list.

— Further developing the communication and cultivation tools to use with donors.

— Laying the groundwork for a future capital campaign.

2007

The top priorities for 2007 will be 1) to keep the individual donor program running while 2) increasing the amount of face-to-face solicitations with major donor prospects. Also, a third goal will be 3) exploring how to create one major annual fundraising event that secures corporate sponsorships and additional individual gifts.

Key additions will be:

— Increasing the dollar amount of the annual campaign.

— Training the board with the help of an outside expert how to do a face-to-face donor solicitations.

— Developing more events specifically to cultivate major donors.

— Creating a plan for a major annual fundraising event.

SAMPLE—BOARD INTRODUCTION LETTER

Dear (first name):

I'm writing to let you know about a wonderful organization called Ultra Nonprofit that provides meaningful, creative work opportunities for low-income young women. These young women gain life, leadership, and job skills through hands-on paid programs.

I have just joined the Ultra Nonprofit board of directors and am very excited to be a part of the work this organization is doing. I have included some information about Ultra Nonprofit because I'd like you to know about their work and hope that you will join me in supporting the young women whose lives are changed through Ultra Nonprofit programs.

Each year, Ultra Nonprofit serves 200 girls ages 14-18 primarily from San Jose's lowest income neighborhoods. Many of our young women face significant challenges, including teen parenthood, homelessness, and exposure to community and domestic violence.

Young women come to our offices two to four days a week after school; programs last between eight and sixteen weeks. Programs combine tangible skill-building (computer proficiency, public speaking, research and writing) with life skills development. All of our programs culminate in the group creation of a product—to date a website, a health book, neighborhood resource guides, and speaker series—all written by young women.

Ultra Nonprofit has generated some compelling measurable results. Over half of our young women participate in more than one program; almost all access additional services, including college prep, career exploration workshops, and academic assistance. Our programs have an 82% completion rate; average attendance is 88%.

Our programs have lasting impact. Eighty percent of graduating seniors go on to college, 26% to a four-year college. Equally important: young women rely on Ultra Nonprofit as a safe, supportive space to "hang out" long after their programs are over. We encourage this. Our motto is "Once an Ultra Nonprofit girl, Always an Ultra Nonprofit girl!"

I've enclosed a copy of Ultra Nonprofit's newsletter, which contains some excellent stories about the young women in our programs, and I've also enclosed an envelope in case you are so moved that you would like to send a contribution to support this work.

I promise to keep in touch with you throughout the year to let you know about Ultra Nonprofit and my participation in its efforts to make life better for low-income young women. I'm already planning to host a get-to-know-Ultra Nonprofit party in May and will be sending out invitations in April!

Thanks for taking time to look at what we do.

Sincerely,

Gloria Fundrazor
Ultra Nonprofit Board of Directors

SAMPLE—DONOR PROSPECT FORM

Our Nonprofit Donor Prospects

_____
Your Name

_____
Prospect Name

_____
Address

_____
Phone

_____
Email

How do you know this person? _____

Have you told this person about Our Nonprofit before? _____

What size gift might this person be capable of giving? _____

_____
Prospect Name

_____
Address

_____
Phone

_____
Email

How do you know this person? _____

Have you told this person about Our Nonprofit before? _____

What size gift might this person be capable of giving? _____

Basic Donor Research

When it comes time to separate major donor prospects from ordinary donor prospects, having done some research about the major donors can give you more confidence about how much to ask for and how to go about asking. Most small nonprofits can't afford to hire a full-time staff person who can do donor research. You can, however, access available resources via the Internet and your local library that will help you with your most important donor prospects. Two of the key uses for this research are determining what the donor's interests are and how much money would be appropriate to ask for.

By doing research to gather basic information about your prospective donor, you can create a profile for the donor's file that you can refer to later as you are getting to know the donor. The information contained in the profile will help you determine the best ways to cultivate the donor, how much money to ask the donor to contribute, and how best to acknowledge the donor's support.

The following is an example of a major donor profile.

Ultra Nonprofit
Confidential Major Donor Research Profile

Prospect: Mr. X

Executive Summary:

Mr. X, approximately age 48 in 2004, retired from the XYZ Corporation of Sunnyvale, CA in the winter of 2003 but remains on the board of directors. He had served as ZYZ's president, chief executive officer and director since he co-founded the company with Mr. G in December of 1982. The company went public in June of 1996. Mr. X and Mr. G both had worked for ABC Inc., a Redwood City wireless communications company, and the two were XYZ's largest stockholders, each holding more than 3.6 million shares before the initial public offering. Each was registered to sell 375,000 shares in the offering.

Residence:

Per xx:
56 Mountain Road
Sidewood, CA 94062-3613
Per San Mateo County tax assessment office web site, property at 56 Mountain Road in Sidewood, CA owned by the xxx Trust, has a net value of $3,631,370 for the assessment year 2000.

Per Yahoo real estate web site and Palo Alto Weekly, property at 56 Mountain Road, Sidewood, CA was purchased for $3,425,000 in 1996 by Mr. X.

Mr. X serves on the advisory board of Sunnyside University. The board bi-ography indicates that Mr. X "lives in Los Altos Hills with his wife and four children." Mr. X may have lived in Los Altos Hills prior to 1996.

Family Information:

Mr. X is married to Diana Y. They have four children: Randolphy, Simon, Jennifer, and Jordan.

Education and Educational Affiliations:

Per XYZ Corp. 10/20/00 proxy, Mr. X. received his BS degree in electrical engineering from the University of California at Los Angeles and his MBA degree from Sunnyside University. He serves on Sunnyside University's advisory board.

Current Business Information:

Mr. X is a director of XYZ Corporation.
Mr. X has a 50% general partner interest in Biotech Associates, a California general partnership.

Mr. X is president and director of Fireside Corporation, a Nevada corporation.

Per Hoover's Online:
XYZ Corporation
99 Bay Drive
Sunnyvale, CA 95134
Phone:
Fax:
Website:

XYZ Corporation helps telecommunications providers offer faster Internet access. Its customizable ABC 2000 (about 86% of sales) lets networks with standard transmission lines, T1 and E1 lines, bound into broadband links of up to 600Mbps and increase transmission, thus making access to multiple communications services. XYZ Corp. is developing products for fault and configuration management, WAN monitoring, and an increased switching capacity over the 2000 system. About 64% of sales come from corporate customers LMN, BBC, CZY, and CDC Corporation.

Career History:

Per XYZ Corp. 10/28/00 proxy report, Mr. X, age 48, was president, chief executive officer and director (since 1982) of XYZ Corp. in Sunnyvale, California. The company went public in June of 1996. XYZ Corporation chief executive officer xxx and chief technical officer xxx co-founded the company in December of 1982. Mr. X and Mr. G both had worked for ABC Inc., a Redwood City wireless communications company, and the two were XYZ's largest stockholders, each holding more than 3.6 million shares before the initial public offering. Each was registered to sell 375,000 shares in the offering.

From 1980 to 1982, Mr. X was vice president of marketing for ABC Electronics, a manufacturer of telephone central office and two-way radio test equipment. From 1975 to 1980, he held various international and domestic sales and marketing management positions for ABC's Telecommunications Division, involved with microwave radio capacity upgrades, telecommunication test equipment, and T-carrier protection and diagnostic systems. Mr. X began his career in telecommunications as an installer, project engineer and transmission engineer with GTW Sylvania in 1971.

Other Affiliations:

Mr. X currently holds the position of chairman of the board of the Telewaddle Industries Association. In addition, he has been a governor of the Electronic Widget Association (EIA) since 1992, and presently is a member of its executive committee.

Executive Compensation:

Per XYZ Corp. 5/27/99 proxy:

In fiscal year 1998, Mr. X's salary was $545,000, plus other compensation which totaled $85,000 (life insurance premiums, retirement benefits, reimbursement of medical expenses, automobile lease or allowance, and operating expenses paid by the company). In FY97, Mr. X's salary was $400,000, plus other compensation which totaled $30,000. In FY96, Mr. X's salary was $345,000, plus other compensation of $76,000.

Other possible compensation:

Mr. X is a director of XYZ Corporation and Fireside Corporation. Presumably all companies offer directors stock options. Some companies also offer directors cash compensation.

Disclosed Stock Holdings:

It is not possible to find all of a prospect's stock holdings—only the ones that he/she is legally required to disclose to the Securities and Exchange Commission (SEC). Directors, top officers, and "insiders" are required to disclose their holdings, and this is publicly available information. However, a prospect can hold substantial amounts of stock in a company and not meet the disclosure requirements (as long as their holdings represent less than 5% of total outstanding stock). For this reason, Mr. X may own additional stock that is not subject to SEC disclosure.

Per XYZ Corporation 5/27/99 proxy statement:

As of 5/10/99, Mr. X beneficially owned 3,084,752 share (21.9%) of XYZ common stock. This includes 1,321,000 shares owned by x, individually, and by xx and xy, or their successors, Trustees U/A dated 12/09/88; 1,050 shares owned by Biotech Associates, a California general partnership in which Mr. X has a 50% general partner interest; 746,208 shares owned by trusts for minor children of Mr. X and 1,000,000 shares owned by Fireside Corporation, a Nevada corporation of which Mr. X is a Director and beneficial ownership as to 746,208 of these shares. Also includes options to purchase 15,625 shares exercisable within 60 days of May 10, 1999. XYZ Corporation stock closed at $12.512 per share on 9/13/99.

Recent Stock Transactions

Per Yahoo Insider Trading:

On 7/29/99 Mr. X gave as a gift 5,000 shares of indirectly held XYZ common stock valued at $14,375

On 12/24/98 Mr. X gave as a gift 1,000 shares of indirectly held XYZ common stock valued at $3,750

On 9/12/98 Mr. X sold 25,000 shares of indirectly held XYZ common stock valued at $150,000

Philanthropy:

It is not possible to find all of a prospect's philanthropy, indeed, sometimes it is not possible to find any of it. Sources of philanthropy include donor listings collections of annual reports and periodicals, as well as searches on the Internet.

5/20/98 per Sunnyside University web site:
The dean of Sunnyside University announced that advisory board members xx, yy, and zz kicked off a challenge to the board to raise funds for the new Center for Innovation by donating over $450,000 themselves.

Per Tech Museum web site:
As of 8/99 XYZ Corporation contributed to the Tech Museum of Innovation in San Jose at the $1,000-2,499 level.

Another tool you need to create before you launch an individual donor program is tiers for gifts that describe the different levels of giving available and the benefits associated with each level. Doing this helps you control the giving process more, communicate more clearly with donors about how they'll be rewarded for giving, and guide these donors toward higher levels of giving over time.

SAMPLE—DONOR BENEFITS LEVELS

Donate to Ultra Nonprofit and equip low-income young women with the life, leadership, and job skills they need to succeed.

Donation Level

Hero $5,000 and above

o   Personalized reports from young women
o   All other benefits below

Role Model $2,500 to $4,999

o   Complimentary ticket to BIG EVENT
o   Major donor dinner party
o   All other benefits below

Mentor $1,000 to $2,499

o   Copies of projects created by young women
o   All other benefits below

Coach $500 to $999

o   Copy of the book
o   Invitation to special private Ultra Nonprofit events
o   All other benefits below

Tutor $126 to $499

o   Invitations to graduation
o   Tour of Ultra Nonprofit office during program
o   Newsletter

Friend up to $125

o   Newsetter

CHAPTER FOUR—
CULTIVATION

ONCE you have identified your donor prospects, the next step is to tell them about your organization and to make them feel connected to it. This process is known in the fundraising field as "donor cultivation." Why do we use the term "cultivation" for this process? Well, cultivating a donor is a little like cultivating a crop—you give your crop attention, water, food, sunlight, all the things it needs to thrive, and then, one day, it produces a bountiful HARVEST! With an individual donor, you give him or her attention, information, invitations to events, answers to questions, personal involvement, and then, one day, your donor produces a bountiful GIFT! Cultivating a donor is the process of nurturing a relationship with him or her toward the goal of receiving a gift.

HOT TIP

GOOD CULTI-
VATION IS PER-
SONALIZED TO
THE INDIVIDUAL
DONOR PROSPECT

As stated earlier, all fundraising is based on relationships between people. Even corporate, government, and foundation funding is based on relationships, however, with individuals, it's all about relationships. A relationship between a donor and an organization grows through the process of cultivation. The process is all about developing, deepening, and strengthening the relationship between a donor and an organization. The key to good cultivation is that it is personalized to each donor and that you scale it to the person's ability to give larger gifts. You invest more time and resources with a donor who has the capacity to give more money. Both staff members and board members participate in the cultivation process. Sometimes the staff takes the lead, and sometimes the board does. In addition, cultivation takes place continuously and on an ongoing basis.

TROPHY CASE

Good cultivation allows you to come to know your donors as they get to know your organization. When you're aware of a donor's particular interests and passions, you can be ready to act when an opportunity arises. For example, I raised the majority of funds for what became an Academy-Award-winning film about an organization by connecting a key donor to the project. I had long known that the donor's biggest dream was to see a film get made about the organization's work. I invited the donor to lunch with prospective filmmakers who wanted to document our work. After lunch, he donated $72,000 to the film.

Chances are very good that you are already engaged in donor cultivation. If you send even one piece of mail to your donors each year, whether it be a postcard to an event or a newsletter, you are doing cultivation. Make an inventory of the specific ways you cultivate donors and prospects because you are going to refine your current activities and build new activities into your program. To do that, you need to know where

TROPHY CASE

I found a special way to cultivate donors to an international nonprofit serving children. While on vacation in Seattle, I kept seeing posters for a book by a local photographer. The exhibit featured his unique photographic portraits of people in Tibet. Finally, I was able to lay my hands on the book in a store. His wonderful photos had such a luminous, other-worldly quality that somehow also managed to bring the people's personalities vividly to life. I tracked him down and proposed his working with us to create a book of portraits of our volunteers and the children they served around the world. Two years later, the photo book was published and offered as a thank you gift to donors.

you are starting from. Cultivation can include mailings, invitations to events, phone calls to say thank you, invitations to visit your program, special reports tailored to the donor's interest, and so on. There are many other ways to cultivate—ways that are limited only by your imagination.

Some potential cultivation techniques can include:
- thanking donors on your organization's website
- making special signage to thank donors at events
- adding more mailings to your annual donor contact, including, for example, a newsletter
- sending email updates to your donors
- having your board members check in with people directly on a regular basis
- asking your donors to participate in occasional surveys about organizational focus or performance

- inviting donors to an exclusive party at some-one's home
- inviting donors to serve on a committee or on your board of directors
- thanking your donors in writing, verbally, publicly, any way you can

One key to successful donor cultivation is to have a proto-col in place that defines how you will process incoming gifts, enter data in a database to manage it, and pinpoint who is responsible for steps involved with managing the data and ac-knowledging the donors. The database is also the place where you keep track of all the cultivation your donor prospects have already received or are scheduled to receive. Here is a sample protocol to show you how many details are involved in this key process that is often dealt with as an afterthought.

SAMPLE—PROTOCOL FOR DONOR GIFT PROCESSING

1) Director of Development opens donation envelopes on the day they arrive and makes a copy of all gifts for her own files

2) Director of Development notes on each check or credit card gift whether the gift is individual, foundation, or corporate and gives to Database Manager the day they arrive; Director of Development shows foundation checks and any documentation to Executive Director

3) If the donor was a prospect of a board member, Director of Development emails the board member to let them know of the gift within 48 hours of our receiving the check

4) Database Manager fills out a deposit slip for checks on Wednesday of each week

5) Database Manager copies checks for herself and makes a copy of the deposit slip and attaches it to the copy of the checks; they are then placed in a three-ring binder that will contain all the copies for the year on Wednesday of each week; there will be one binder for individual gifts, and a second one for foundation and corporate gifts

6) Database Manager takes the deposit to the bank on Wednesday of each week

7) Database Manager calls in credit card gifts on Thursday of each week

8) Database Manager enters all data from checks and credit card gifts into Ultra Nonprofit database and captures as much information as possible, including spouse's name, phone number, email address, special instructions, etc. on Thursday of each week

9) Database Manager prepares a formal acknowledgment letter for donor contributions every Friday for all checks received that week. The exception is in the case of BIG EVENT acknowledgements, which are done in one batch no later than one week after the BIG EVENT

10) Director of Development reviews and writes the standard acknowledgement letter twice per year, once before the spring direct mailing and once before the year-end direct mailing and gives the copy to Database Manager at least two weeks before the mailing goes to press

11) Database Manager produces the donor acknowledgement letters and puts them in a folder for Anne to review before they are mailed.

12) Executive Director reads all of the letters in the folder and notes any changes within 24 hours of receiving the folder

13) Database Manager makes a copy of the acknowledgement letters and places them in a three-ring binder for all individual gifts for this fiscal year the day they are mailed

14) Database Manager notes each gift from donor, amount, and date on a running chart on the inside cover of this three-ring binder on the day they are mailed

15) Director of Development prepares a list of major donors who need personal thank you cards and emails the list to Anne within 24 hours of receiving their gifts

16) Executive Director selects who she will write to from the list (within one week) and lets Director of Development know immediately

17) Director of Development writes the remaining thank you cards within one week

18) Once per month, Director of Development and Database Manager look at a report of donations from the database and compare it to a report

from our bookkeeping program to reconcile the numbers; this should be done before any upcoming board meeting, ideally one week before financial data are emailed to board members

19) If a holiday falls in this process, then each step will be done on the next possible business day.

20) All donation information is neatly and promptly filed in binders, folders, and filing cabinets; donor information is sensitive and should only be accessible to administrative staff.

The following examples include acknowledgment letters and an introductory letter for new donor prospects.

SAMPLE—ACKNOWLEDGMENT LETTER ONE

July 3, 2002

Patty Johnson
86 Shore Road
Alviso, CA 95021

Dear Ms. Johnson:

We are very pleased that Donor One and Donor Two have introduced Ultra Nonprofit to you. We are even more excited and pleased that you have decided to become a part of the important work we are doing to provide meaningful work and leadership opportunities for low-income young women. Thank you so much for your contribution of $1,000 to Ultra Nonprofit.

Your contribution will really make a difference in Ultra Nonprofit's ability to provide low-income young women real jobs with real pay, to provide them with college-preparatory support, and to develop their leadership, public-speaking, job management, and technical skills.

We will continue to be in touch with you as Ultra Nonprofit expands its programs and involves even more young women. We are certain that there will be many success stories to share thanks to the generosity of committed Ultra Nonprofit supporters like you.

Thank you for the positive opportunities you help make possible for low-income young women.

Sincerely,

Deborah Director
Ultra Nonprofit Executive Director

Note: No goods or services were traded in return for your contribution of $1,000.00. You should keep this receipt with your tax records. Tax ID #

July 2, 2002

Kathleen Brown
457 Collins Street
San Francisco, CA 94110

Dear Ms. Brown:

On behalf of everyone at Ultra Nonprofit, I would like to thank you for your generous donation of $250. Your support allows us to continue our work empowering young women and expanding their economic opportunities.

With your funding, we will continue our efforts to serve more young women through our programs. In addition, we will rely on the generous support of donors like you to provide low-income young women with career, college, and life planning services through Bound for Success.

We look forward to an exciting year at Ultra Nonprofit, and are highly appreciative of your assistance. Thank you so much for your help.

Sincerely,

Deborah Director
Executive Director

Note: No goods or services were traded in return for your contribution of $250. You should keep this receipt with your tax records. Tax ID#

SAMPLE—
BOARD INVITATION LETTER OR EMAIL FOR CULTIVATION

Hey there!

I'm sending you an invitation to a special event designed to connect you with interesting people and with a fantastic nonprofit organization called This Great Nonprofit.

I joined the board of TGN because I am impressed with the work of the organization, and, as a former educator who has worked closely with adolescent girls, I see what a tremendous, positive impact TGN's programs have for the girls who participate in them.

The girls who experience our programs write about their experiences in such a way that you know they have been changed forever. Many of these girls come to us "at-risk." They leave the program with a real sense of self, a deep-down confidence in their abilities, and they bring this energy back to the communities they are from, touching everyone they know with their renewed spirit.

We're hosting a fundraising event for TGN on Wednesday, August 8. An interesting assortment of people from high-tech, nonprofit, and other fields will be our guests for the evening, which will include lots of time to mix and mingle. During the event, we'll give a very short presentation on TGN.

I hope you will join us for some fun and feel-good involvement. A suggested donation is described below. You can mail contributions in the form of a check made payable to TGN. Send them to me, or make your gift at the event.

Call me to RSVP. And bring your friends!

CHAPTER FIVE—
DIRECT MAIL

THE important thing to know about direct mail is that it is the simplest and most important piece of the start-up individual giving program. Most organizations will start off their individual giving program by writing and mailing one direct mail solicitation letter to most if not all of their donors and prospects at the end of the year. If you send a letter at the end of the year, you will take advantage of people's feelings of holiday cheer and generosity as well as their desire to make more donations that they can write off of their taxes before the year runs out. A good direct mail appeal letter will be short and straightforward in its request, and it will provide an envelope that donors can use to mail a gift back to you.

Some other things to add to this device to make it even more effective include:

- A challenge gift that promises to match gifts made in response to the letter

- A deadline by which gifts are needed to earn a challenge gift

- A personal appeal by someone who is actually served by the programs of the organization

- A photograph to bring the mission of the organization alive

- A focus on the reader of the letter through the use of the word "you" throughout the letter

- A very specific request for a gift—"Your gift of $50, $100, or more by January 1..."

- A preprinted response envelope that includes suggested levels for gifts

- An option on the preprinted envelope for donors to make their gift by credit card or by gift of stock if you are set up to receive these types of gifts

- Selective use of bold-face type to make key words stand out throughout the letter; but beware of over-using this technique or it will make the letter harder to read

- A P.S. below the signature—studies have shown that people read the first line of a letter and P.S. even it they read nothing else! Repeat your request in the P.S., and you are in business!

HOT TIP

EVERY INDIVIDUAL GIVING PROGRAM SHOULD USE DIRECT MAIL

Once you establish a year-end direct mail appeal letter, you can add a second appeal letter in the spring, or multiple letters throughout the year. Bear in mind that donors can quickly go from feeling connected to the organization and inspired to give to feeling over-saturated and harassed by receiving too many letters.

There are a few ways to make your direct mail program cost-effective. One of them is to calculate how many pieces of mail you will send throughout the year and to preprint all of your stationery, remits, and envelopes at the beginning of the year. Once they are printed, you can often arrange to store them at your printer's warehouse until they are needed.

By printing in quantity, you will reap the reward of volume discounts. Whenever possible, and that should be most of the time, plan to mail your letters by nonprofit bulk mail presorted rates which will give you substantial savings on postage rates. Alternatively, you may be able to solicit a donation of postage from a corporate or individual sponsor who will agree to run the letters through their postage meter as a donation. Plan to seek out this kind of donation far in advance of when you are planning to do your mailing.

One of the keys to running a successful direct mail program is to maintain your data in an orderly, professional way. For smaller nonprofits, creating your own donor database using FileMaker Pro software will offer you maximum flexibility for a minimal cost over other software packages specifically designed for donor data management. FileMaker Pro is compatible with Macintosh computers. Many nonprofits that are on a PC platform swear by Raiser's Edge, another respected program that does a good job of keeping your donor information where you need it and allows you to get the reports you want.

I have included a variety of sample direct mail letters for you to borrow and learn from. One of the most important things for you to know about direct mail is that you must be flexible and learn from mistakes. Experiment with small changes and new features in your letters, and see if they result in more gifts.

The following is a sample direct mail strategy developed for a large nonprofit organization that, while it had been in operation for 85 years, had never before used direct mail. A smaller, younger nonprofit organization could use a similar approach to launch a direct mail program and get results fast.

COMMUNITY WORKS 2006-2007 DIRECT MAIL STRATEGY

Overview

In 2006, Community Works will establish a regular, "routinized" direct mail program. This strategy outlines a suggested approach to using the direct mail program not only to raise dollars, but also to create relationships with donors. You should try to keep the same routine in place for at least two full years in order to "train" your donors to expect certain pieces by mail and by email and also to develop their giving habits. After two years, decide what is working and what is not and make adjustments accordingly.

Type of printed pieces

The direct mail program will incorporate three types of print materials:

1) Letters

Letters are the key device to secure gifts. Letters need to be tight, well designed, and direct. Messages should be focused—you don't want too many angles or competing points to dilute the main message of the "ask." Keep each letter to one page.

I recommend sending two letters in 2006, one in the spring in mid-March and one in the fall just before Thanksgiving. The fall letter capitalizes on the traditional season of charitable giving. Whatever else you do with other appeal letters, you want to send the fall letter. The spring letter gives donors who did not give in the fall a second chance to give. It also gives donors who have given a chance to increase their giving. A standard letter-sized appeal without any special design needs is a perfect candidate for full-color online printing at very cheap rates.

2) Newsletter

A newsletter can be a simple two-page sheet, front and back, or something more elaborate, either a four-page or eight-page piece. The goal of the newsletter is to communicate the human story of what Community Works does without including any kind of hard ask. In a four-page or eight-page newsletter, you can staple a remit envelope in the center of the piece. However, I would caution not to expect many returns—this is the nature of a newsletter; it's too indirect to create the kind of response you get from a direct mail letter. What the newsletter accomplishes is to present human stories and photos that put a face on what you do and what your mission is. The newsletter does not have to be elaborate, but it does need to be well designed, engaging, and attractive. The newsletter is a very good candidate for full-color online printing at very cheap rates.

3) Postcards

Postcards are a kind of "filler" that you can use to make special announcements to donors; they can announce a sale, a breakthrough or milestone with a program, or an open house or other event that you want people to attend. Postcards help reinforce your messages in between more expensive and involved printed pieces. It creates more impressions, cheaply. You can create one uniform postcard design and print it online in huge bulk quantities, then take batches to the local print shop for imprinting with special messages as you need them. This gives you a uniform look that becomes familiar to donors (think branding) but saves you big dollars on printing.

Suggested timeframe

Here's one potential calendar for all of your mailings and emails:

Jan	Feb	Mar	Apr	May	June	Jul	Aug	Sept	Oct	Nov	Dec
Email	Newsletter	Spring Direct mail	Card	Email	Card	Email	Card	Newsletter	Email	Fall Direct mail	Email & card

I recommend sending both an email and a postcard in December to rally donors to respond to the November direct mail appeal and the fall campaign by the year-end. The email and postcard can reinforce the ask, give an update on the money raised, and remind of the year-end deadline. You may not have enough time to get a newsletter created, printed, and mailed by February 2006; instead, skip that step for this spring and focus on getting a newsletter prepared for the fall. You can then create the following newsletter for spring 2007. If you want to save money, in the summer months, skip the extra postcard mailings and do emails instead; since many people are traveling in the summer, this may work just as well or better.

Content of letters

Your first goal is to finalize and refine the overall Community Works messaging you plan to use in all of your marketing. You want to select a different theme for each direct mail letter that you send out. While each letter can reinforce other messages, it needs to have one main message. You should continue to build and expand on the theme of transformation we used in the fall 2005 letter since it's so strong and allows you to play off the transformation Community Works is undergoing while you transform people's lives. Since you are trying to establish what the "new Community Works" is in the donors' minds, each letter can describe one new venture you have launched. Use each new venture to show how you transform people's lives.

Take one appeal letter to focus on:

- truck driving academy
- computer recycling
- E-Store
- Other new ventures or aspects of the organization

The order that you choose to incorporate these ventures in the letters is up to you. Any one of them would work for the spring or fall appeal—however, considering that you have already done some promotion of the computer recycling program, you may want to focus on the other two ventures first.

In general, each appeal letter should be written directly to the reader, using the word "you" frequently, making clear in the first paragraph that the reader is being called on to do something, and concluding with a direct ask for money. Also, every letter should include a P.S. that reinforces your ask, drives the reader to your website, or offers a special reward for giving (i.e., premium, discount coupon, etc.). Never leave out the P.S.

Design and printing

For the spring 2006 direct mail appeal, use a regular letter in a standard envelope. This will significantly cut costs. In the fall, use a specially designed card to create a holiday feel, such as you did for the fall 2005 letter. Aim for repeating design elements—fonts, logos, graphics—that carry across the entire range of print materials you plan to use so that donors come to recognize a printed piece from Community Works. To keep costs down overall, consider putting all of your design and all of your print needs out to bid as a package in the beginning of the year. Get four or five competing bids in order to reduce your costs. Also research possible sources for online printing. I would recommend calling the online printing companies, speaking to someone, and asking for a packet of printing samples so you can check out their paper, the color quality, etc. While you research online printing options for standard-sized letters, postcards, and envelopes, keep in mind that nonstandard pieces will still have to go to the print shop. As I mentioned above, map out all of your print needs for the entire year including timing and quantities. Submit the package to bid with local printers. Compare online costs for the basic pieces. Get the best prices for everything you plan to do.

How email and web tie in

Always put your email and web address on every printed mail piece to continue to drive donors to your website. In time, you can create an email newsletter that could potentially replace your print newsletter. You can also give donors the option of selecting an email newsletter versus the print newsletter once you have perfected the email version and its delivery system. I recommend sending a short email update in every month that does not contain a printed mailing piece going to donors. This fills the gaps and keeps Community Works on everyone's minds in between when you plan to ask directly for money. Your website should include a prominent button on the home page to capture people your direct mail drives to the website who prefer to give online. Don't make them hunt for the link. The home page should also have a prominent way for people to sign up for email updates. The email updates you send out should also have direct links to your donation page on your website so people don't have to type in your address in their browsers. How to deliver the email efficiently and easily is another topic for research.

Donor lists

You need to further clean-up and refine your donor lists. Add the list of people you left out of the fall 2005 mailing and integrate it with your other lists. Decide if the different constituents making up the global list (retail customers, monetary donors, Project Connect, etc.) need slightly different language in their respective letters or if one uniform letter can do the job. Having different messages makes the process slightly harder to manage, but that's why we have mail-merge programs. Also, review what you would need to do to go from a "Dear Friend" letter to personalizing everyone's letters. Look over the pitfalls of not having everyone's first name, preferred salutation, etc. I would suggest going with "Dear Friend" until you have worked out any potential bugs with personalization. Your next step in 2006 will be to ask your board members to each provide you with a list of 40 to 100 personal contacts including address, phone, and emails to integrate into your direct mail program. These individuals should immediately start receiving newsletters, direct mail appeals, and other contact from Community Works. You should have board members identify which of these contacts are prospective major donors before you begin the cultivation process, and you should plan to take further, more personalized steps to cultivate them. In order to keep your mailing lists clean, have the words "address correction requested" printed on your mailings so the post office will provide you with updated information on donors who may have moved. There is a charge per piece for this service, so do it only with smaller pieces, such as postcards, rather than your newsletter.

Upgrading donors

Once you have the program fully established, potentially at the beginning of year two, start customizing your appeals in order to upgrade donor giving. Segment the list based on past gifts. Donors who have given $50 should receive a letter asking them to consider a gift of $75 or $100. Donors who gave $100 should get a letter suggesting $150 or $200, etc. If after two year, donors have not responded to any of your appeals, you should consider trimming your list to save money on printing and mailing. I suggest doing the trimming slowly and carefully since it can take a long time for some people to respond. Give them time. If you are going to cull your list, I recommend combining it with additional acquisition mailings to try to gain some new donors as you slough non-donors off of your list. Also, before dropping someone completely, send them one more customized appeal asking for a gift and asking if they want to continue to receive these mailings—or not.

Major donors versus regular donors

Major donors should not receive the same direct mail appeals that the general mailing list receives. They should get newsletters and postcards and other special mailings, but they should not receive a general letter asking them for support. They should either get a customized letter with a specific dollar request, or they should not be solicited by mail at all. Ideally and ultimately, they should instead get a face-to-face solicitation involving the board member who knows them and a member of your development staff. Given your lack of a relationship with them, all current major donors should be contacted by phone to establish a personal connection. If someone on your board or staff knows an individual major donor, then that person should make the call. If no one in particular knows that donor, then any board member or staff person can call them. The goal of the call is to answer their questions, thank them for past support, and invite them to lunch, to an event, etc. The goal of the call is to establish a relationship.

Challenge gift

One of the best tools for maximizing the outcome of a direct mail appeal is including a challenge gift in it. You need a gift from an individual, a foundation, or a combination of these totaling a significant amount toward your overall campaign goal. I recommend securing a challenge gift for both the spring direct mail campaign as well as the fall direct mail campaign. For example, if your spring goal is $45,000 in direct mail gifts, find a donor or donors who will pledge to give $15,000 if you raise $30,000. This type of campaign structure gives donors confidence, makes them feel excited, and creates a sense of urgency so they give now. The challenge gift can also come from your board of directors. Have one person on your board pledge an amount and ask the rest of the board to match it. Their combined gift can become the challenge gift. There is a very good chance that you will raise far more than your goal when you use a challenge gift. I once used a challenge gift of $50,000 to raise an additional $117,000 in gifts for a total of $167,000 in that campaign. My original goal was $100,000. You can also approach foundations to give this type of gift. The donors who pledge the challenge gift do not actually have to make the gift until you have successfully met the challenge. This makes this type of appeal attractive to them. It guarantees success for everyone involved so long as you structure the campaign in a reasonable way with reasonable goals.

Event tie-ins

Consider hosting an annual open house event or other "drop-in" events to bring donors into face-to-face contact with Community Works. Have special sign-ups and drawings at these events. Everyone who gives you an email address is entered into a drawing for some great door prizes. In any case, cultivation events are another key way to develop relationships with donors. Donors who come to events become repeat contributors through direct mail. Use your postcard mailings, newsletters, and emails to promote the open house event.

Priority To Do List

— Continue to clean donor lists

— Add list left out of fall 2005 mailing

— Finalize marketing messages and design elements

— Solicit lists from board members

— Keep website updated with easy links to donating and signing up for email

— Secure challenge gift for spring 2006 mailing

— Outline components of printing bid package

— Send out RFP to print houses for bids on print package

— Research online printing costs

— Design newsletter, creating template for future issues

— Determine mechanism for sending email bulletins

— Contact major donors to establish relationships

— Secure challenge gift for fall 2006 mailing

— Prepare for 2007 direct mail "cycle"

SAMPLE—DIRECT MAIL APPEAL LETTER ONE

November 15, 2005

Dear Friend,

Because you're a past friend of our organization, this holiday season I invite you to renew your sense of goodwill.

If you're like me, right now you could use some good tidings. We've endured hurricanes, terrorism, and war. We've witnessed the suffering caused by tsunamis, mudslides, and earthquakes. And we've seen the gap between rich and poor yawning wider. Where is the good news? When will things change?

Things are already changing here at Community Works, and that's why I'm writing. I want to renew your sense of hope by telling you about what we are doing to transform lives, communities, and the world.

As I once did, you may believe Community Works is just a bunch of thrift stores. However, I've learned that Community Works is actually far more. We're a nonsectarian non-profit that helps people who have struggled with disabilities, chemical dependency, or lack of skills to find jobs that sustain themselves and their families. By helping them change their lives, Community Works helps transform our entire community.

But I'm excited to say that Community Works is also undergoing a transformation. When I became Community Works's CEO two years ago, we started looking at what we do and how to do it better. Today, we have a new mission, a new structure, and new programs. We are creating cutting-edge training opportunities and jobs through our truck driving academy, a just-launched computer recycling program, and our growing E-store. For an organization that's been around for 85 years, we're showing a knack for innovation.

This is where my invitation extends to you. Community Works is proud that our non-profit enterprises cover more than 85% of our expenses, but we need your help to create yet more jobs, a cleaner environment, and new businesses that give people a reason to hope—and smile.

Please support the transformative work of Community Works with a personal tax-deductible gift of $50, $100, $250, or more by December 31 so we can expand our innovative services in 2006 and reach even more individuals, families and communities. Please use the enclosed remit envelope to send your gift today.

I look forward to staying in touch with you to share future news. I'll be the person bearing some of that longed-for good news! To help me stay in touch, please write your email address on the remit envelope.

For your generous contribution to Community Works, I send my warmest thanks.

Sincerely,

Deborah Daring
President and CEO

P.S.—Visit our website at **www.communityworks.org** to make an online contribution, sign up for email updates, or learn more about the transformation taking place at Community Works.

SAMPLE—DIRECT MAIL APPEAL LETTER TWO

November 20, 2005

Dear Friend of Young Women:

You saw what happened with Hurricane Katrina, how the people that terrible storm hit hardest were those who were poor. Those who couldn't buy a plane ticket. Or a tank of gas. Those who were the last to leave New Orleans. Or the ones left behind. Those stranded at the Superdome or the Convention Center or the nursing homes. Those now scattered like leaves around our country.

You saw the news reports, and you may have wondered how to keep such a terrible scene of human suffering from ever happening again. You may have wondered how we can make sure that poverty never causes another American life to end so senselessly. You may have wondered what to do.

I'm writing to tell you what we can do and how you can help, because I work for Young Women's Center, an organization that attacks this exact problem head on.

Young Women's Center helps young women who deal with the realities of poverty every day. We empower young women in economic terms through meaningful paid work, and we empower them in spirit by believing in their abilities. Because we empower young women, they are going to college, embarking on career paths, and becoming leaders who in turn are improving their communities. This is how to change the future for Americans who live in poverty and for our country as a whole.

I am writing to ask if you can make a personal gift of $50, $100, $250 or more to Young Women's Center to help young women combat and defeat poverty. Please use the enclosed envelope to send a check to Young Women's Center today.

Together, we can make sure that no one is left behind in the next disaster. And, together, we can make sure that no one is left behind in pursuit of the American dream. When people have overcome poverty, they can not only save themselves, they can save others, too.

This time, let's be proactive in dealing with poverty. Thank you so much for your generous support!

Sincerely,

Jerri Jones
Young Women's Center Executive Director

SAMPLE—DIRECT MAIL APPEAL LETTER THREE

Dear Friend of Young Women:

My name is Carrie, and, as a former Ultra Nonprofit program participant and a member of the Ultra Nonprofit Board of Directors, I am writing to ask you to give to Ultra Nonprofit today.

I came to Ultra Nonprofit as a sophomore at Smith High, and I am now attending college. Ultra Nonprofit was the first place that helped me plan for and realize success. And I am not alone.

We all know the economy is still bad and that funding for nonprofits is down. That is why I'm asking for your help. Ultra Nonprofit has kicked off a campaign to raise an additional $75,000 by December 31, 2003. The campaign is starting off with a $20,000 challenge gift. That means every dollar you contribute is twice as powerful.

As someone whose life has changed because of Ultra Nonprofit, I can tell you that this organization helps make the world a better place. With your help, 2004 will see Ultra Nonprofit reaching more low-income young women, not fewer.

On behalf of all the past, present, and future Ultra Nonprofit girls, I want to thank you for your support.

Sincerely,

Carrie Jenkins

P.S. If you make a gift of $250 or more, we will send you a free copy of Ultra Nonprofit, a book by and for young women. Ultra Nonprofit was written by our own participants and recently published by Full Speed Press.

CHAPTER SIX—
HOUSE PARTIES

*T*HIS book deliberately downplays events as a fundraising tool of the individual donor program. Why? Because too many organizations get stuck on doing events and refuse to budge from this position. Boards and staff alike seek comfort and refuge in doing the annual black-tie event or hotel luncheon. Knowing what these events require, it's hard to say why. These types of events are labor intensive, they require the involvement of large numbers of volunteers helping sell tickets, and they tax staff members to the nth degree. Worse yet, nine times out of ten, these events don't raise enough money to justify the costs of putting them on. And all of this continues to happen because nonprofit board and staff can't bring themselves to cultivate donors toward direct solicitation. They cling to doing events because they are afraid to do face-to-face solicitations. In writing this book, I am doing my part to try to break this tragic practice.

However, there is one event that performs yeoman's duty in the successful individual donor program, and that is the house party. This is the only event I will discuss in this book. House parties are a great way to introduce people to an organization and to inspire them to support its work. House parties are a less direct way to ask for money, and because of that, they are often easier to do than a scary "face-to-face ask." House parties are a great way to create an instant personal relationship with donors because the people who attend are responding to a personal invitation from their friend, the host, who is already committed to the organization. The host is very honest about what the party is about, mentioning that it is an opportunity to get to know about an organization that is near and dear to the host's heart and for guests to actually show their support for the organization by making a gift. Guests will come to the party because it is at their friend's house and because a low-key, fun introduction in this type of setting will not be threatening. It will sound fun!

It's a good idea to host house parties throughout the calendar year. The reason for this is that you can continually introduce and cultivate new potential donors during the entire year, not just when you have a major event scheduled or plan to do a year-end appeal. Asking an individual to host a house party is also another great way to cultivate him or her as a donor and all-around supporter and create yet another bond with the organization. Also, house parties are the single best way to convert prospective donors into actual donors—on the spot—by making a mass introduction and mass appeal for gifts.

If your organization is not already doing house parties, then you need to start organizing some today. Make a list of some of your best and most dedicated supporters who have a nice house and a circle of friends. Then, follow this list of steps for a successful house party:

1) Find a host who is willing to host the party and who has a nice house that will showcase the organization well and be a draw for guests.

2) The host should understand that you are asking him or her to pay for catering and drinks. Other expenses may include valet parking (for crowded neighborhoods), decorations, etc. Make sure everyone involved knows what the costs will be and who will be paying for them before you start

working on the event. The host can receive a tax acknowledgement letter for the value of the costs associated with hosting the event.

3) Create a guest list; figure out who the host knows and wants to invite; you can mix in guests from others on the board or have co-hosts to get a big enough attendance; the best house parties are not too big. Shoot for 15 to 30 guests maximum. More than that tends to dilute your connection to the attendees.

4) Set a date; time and day of week will depend on the crowd and what works for them; evening cocktail parties can work for a social crowd, afternoon Sunday teas can work for people who like quieter affairs or who are just too busy during the week.

5) Create a simple invitation; On the invite, state that the event is a benefit and get-to-know gathering for the organization and its mission; state that guests will be asked to support the organization with a personal contribution.

6) Send the invitations with the host's name on return address. RSVP in the invitation should have a call-by date. Can have guests RSVP to an office, or call the host directly.

7) By RSVP date, check who has not responded. Host should call to follow up no-calls and encourage people to come.

8) At the event, most of the time is spent with everybody mingling and having a good time. About halfway through, gather everyone to give them a 10-minute presentation about the organization. Keep it brief. Tell them what you do and how wonderful it is. Then, the host takes over and says how great he or she thinks the organization is—great enough to write a check to support the organization's work. If the host wants to make a gift on the spot, she should hand her check to a representative of the organization and then ask everyone at the event to get out their checkbooks and write their own check right there. You should have some

plants in the audience who then come up to hand in their checks. The host thanks everyone and says you'll keep in touch about the continuing good work. The party continues after this stage as long as guests want to stay.

9) Follow up the event with a thank you to everyone who came and gave. Send a different letter to those who came but didn't give, telling them there's still time. Send a third letter to those who could not attend telling them how great the event was, what a shame it was they missed it, but telling them they can still be part of the excitement by writing a check.

That's it. If you follow this basic outline, you should have a great fundraiser. You should continue to cultivate everyone from the guest list and pay especial attention to anybody who expresses outstanding interest or who gives a large check.

Another variation on the house party is a corporate office party. This type of event is similar to the house party except it usually takes place at a place of business, either during the work day, such as over lunch or after the work day.

SAMPLE—HOUSE PARTY FOLLOW UP LETTER ONE

August 27, 2001

Dear Friend of Our Org:

We'd like to thank all of you who joined us on August 8 for a wonderful evening in support of Our Org and their programs for adolescent girls. The donated space provided a fantastic venue to meet, mingle, and learn about this worthwhile charity and the work they do. The food and wine were great, and the company assembled was even better.

For those of you who made a contribution at the event, we want to extend our warmest personal thanks for your generosity. As the story of Mary, Our Org program graduate, proved, it is possible for a short but intense wilderness experience to change a girl's life forever.

For those of you who were not able to join us, or who did not make a contribution at the event, there is still time for you to give your support.

The Our Org board has accepted the challenge of raising $20,000 toward a total goal of $60,000. Every gift counts in helping us reach our goal. We hope that you will choose to make a contribution between $40 and $200 today. Please send your checks to the address shown below. And thank you in advance for becoming part of Our Org!

We promise to let all of you know—whether you attended the event or not—how we do in reaching our goal. And we also promise to keep you informed about how your support makes real learning, growth, and personal blossoming possible for the girls in this year's program.

On behalf of the girls and their ascent through courage, we thank you!

Sincerely,

Sally Smith and Jenny Jones
Our Org Board of Directors

SAMPLE—HOUSE PARTY FOLLOW UP LETTER TWO

February 12, 2003

Dear Friend of Our Org:

We are sorry you weren't able to join us yesterday for the tea party graciously hosted on our behalf by Nancy and Christy Smith. We're writing to let you know what happened at the event and to share some information about Our Org with you. We have enclosed a package of information that includes a book created by our young women, our latest newsletter, and two brochures describing our programs.

A group of 13 people joined us yesterday at the Smith's house for a short presentation about Our Org, a San Francisco nonprofit organization that has been in operation since 1998. For many of our young women, Our Org is the only safe environment they know. Because our services are long-term and time-intensive, Our Org enables young women to develop lasting relationships that nurture their self-esteem and sense of confidence. As we like to say around the office, "Once an Our Org girl, ALWAYS an Our Org girl!"

As we mentioned at the party, 2003 will be a challenging year financially for Our Org. Due to the continuing decline of the stock market, we must reach out to individuals who care about our work and want to see it continue.

We hope that you will become an Our Org supporter today. Your contribution of $50, $100, $250 or more will enable us to continue to serve the same number of young women this year, without having to scale back. In exchange for your support, I promise to stay in touch with you throughout the year, letting you know about the personal success stories of some of the individual girls we serve. Thank you in advance for helping make these inspiring stories possible!

Sincerely,

Deborah Director
Our Org Executive Director

CHAPTER SEVEN—
SOLICITATION

*T*HE eventual goal of all the donor cultivation you engage in with your prospects is to go face to face to ask for a specific contribution. The term in the fundraising field for this face-to-face meeting is a "solicitation" meeting. You are there to solicit the support of the individual you have forged a relationship with and have involved in your organization. In order to be successful, the solicitation meeting needs to follow certain rules—not hard and fast ones, but rules of thumb.

Once you have formed a relationship with the donor prospect through mailings, events, and special communications, you are on your way to being able to conduct the solicitation. You will know it is time to do a solicitation if the donor has expressed interest in the organization's work, has gotten more involved in this work, has made a contribution, and has asked you to communicate with him or her about particular interests. While the donor has made a contribution, he or she most likely has not made a gift that is commensurate with his or her ability to give. In short, this prospect has the ability to give much more.

You will know that the prospect has the ability to give much more based on two things. First, the board member who has introduced this prospect to the board knows the person well and is familiar with his or her giving to other organizations or is familiar with his or her work situation and general life-style. Your board member can tell you that the donor lives in a 20,000 square-foot mansion and has a vacation home in Tahiti. This tells you that the $250 gift he gave in response to your last direct mail piece is probably not all he can do. Second, you have done some Internet or library-based research about the donor and have discovered that his home sold for $4.3 million in its last sale, that he gave to several political campaigns and to several nonprofit organizations at a specific level, and that he owns his own business that is about to go public. All of these pieces of information tell you that you can ask the donor for a specific amount of money. While they don't give you a scientific gauge of how much to ask for, they can help you arrive at a ballpark figure.

HOT TIP

RESEARCH AND COMMON SENSE WILL HELP DETERMINE HOW MUCH TO ASK A DONOR TO GIVE

TROPHY CASE

A board member and I were five minutes from meeting with our biggest donor who gave $100,000 each year. We had agreed earlier to ask her for $500,000, but now the board member got cold feet and insisted we ask for less. When we did our solicitation meeting, I asked the donor for $200,000—and she didn't even blink. Her easy response told me we had asked her for too little. The good news? It's all cultivation. That same donor's next gift was $5 million.

If you are the staff person for the organization, you will suggest a figure to the board member who knows this prospect and who'll go on the solicitation meeting with you. If the board member feels good about the amount, you are probably on the right track. Generally, you want to ask a donor for about twice as much as you hope or expect to receive as a result of the solicitation. The reason for this is that you want to ask in a way that "stretches" the donor's ability to give. The fact is, people are always likely to give less rather than more. To get more, you have to "stretch" them!

HOT TIP

IT'S ALWAYS
BETTER TO HAVE
THE BOARD
MEMBER SET UP
THE MEETING

You want to reserve the solicitation meeting for larger donors, or people who have the capacity to become larger donors. You don't want to waste your time and resources meeting with people who can give no more than $250 if that is the most they can do and a direct mail appeal letter is likely to net that result. You do want to meet with people who have the capacity to give more because they are not likely to give it unless you take the time to meet with them in person. The face-to-face meeting focuses everyone's attention. It sends a message that you have something important to talk about. There will be no distractions or evasions. In order to set up this meeting, the staff member and the board member of the organization need to discuss their strategy. Is this prospect ready to be solicited? How much have they given to date? How much should we ask them for in the meeting? What special interests does this person have? Will there be any specific questions this person will have or objections she will raise? Should we ask for a general support gift, or should we offer to apply this gift to something specific that will really resonate with this donor?

Once the staff member and the board member agree to the

basic facts of how the solicitation will be done, then the board member takes responsibility for setting up a meeting with this individual prospect. The reason that the board member sets up the meeting and not the staff person is because the prospect, who is a friend of the board member, will have a much harder time ignoring or turning down the board member than he will the staff member who is a total stranger paid to get his money. The board member calls and tells the person that he wants to meet with him in order to update him on the organization and to ask for his support. If the donor prospect evades, seeks to

HOT TIP

ASK FOR AT LEAST TWO TIMES WHAT YOU HOPE TO RECEIVE

find out an amount for the gift request, or stalls, then the board member must press for a meeting. This can take some patience and persistence, and a board member needs to be coached to hang in there with a prospect who may squirm. The board member should offer to be flexible in setting up the meeting, trying to arrange it according to the prospect's schedule and preference for a meeting location. Be prepared to meet before work, during work, or even after work, if that is necessary in order to get the face-to-face meeting with this prospect. If time is an issue, negotiate to keep it short.

As we have already discussed, one of the main reasons why people are afraid to do a face-to-face donor solicitation is because the individual may say "No" to the request. To be perfectly honest, people are likely to say no. In fact, the general rule of thumb in fundraising is that you should expect to hear two no's before you hear a yes from a donor. So it's not so important to worry about hearing the no. The more important question is what to do when the no happens. I have always approached this question by looking into what lies behind the word no. I call this "dissecting the no." No really doesn't mean never. It usually means one of several things. It can mean "No, not now." Right now might not be the best time for this individual to make a gift. In that case, your job is to find out when would be a good time. Sometimes no means, "No, not that amount." In that case, your job is to ask what amount would work for this person. Generally, because you are asking for more than you expect to receive from this person, you will hear this kind of no. Sometimes, no means, "No, because I still don't know enough or I have some reservations about what you just told me." Then, you need to address those concerns. No rarely means flat-out no. It usually means "Maybe, if you answer this question or that question."

You can increase your success in a donor meeting by coming to the meeting prepared for all kinds of different versions of

HOT TIP

"NO" DOESN'T ALWAYS MEAN "NO"—YOU NEED TO LEARN TO READ BETWEEN THE LINES

no. Anticipate what the donor may object to or how she will respond and be rehearsed in your response. You will significantly increase your chances of coming away with a yes. Even after all the preparation in the world, the truth will still remain that you will not be able to know the outcome of the request.

There's only one way to find out—and that's to ask.

What happens in the solicitation meeting?

It's time to prepare for a direct donor solicitation when the individual has been cultivated and has shown some interest in the organization and its mission. It's also time when you have done some research about the individual's ability to give a major gift and you feel that he or she will give more if you go and ask directly.

Usually—and ideally—the meeting doesn't feel like a meeting. It should have a friendly, laid-back tone, and it is the job of the board member to make sure this happens. There's no use in jumping right into business. This is your friend, after all! Start off by stating how much you appreciate your friend's having made the time to meet and reaffirm your commitment to sticking to the agreed-upon time length for the meeting. Check in with your friend, asking about what's new, how the family is, how that last trip to Palm Springs went, etc. Once you have established a rapport and have set a relaxed tone, then you, the board member, can shift the topic of conversation to the organization. Reiterate that you have asked for this meeting because you believe in this organization and

HOT TIP

THE BOARD MEMBER TALKS ABOUT HIS PERSONAL INVOLVEMENT AND FEELING FOR THE ORGANIZATION

would like your friend to support it, too. Some good ways to illustrate your involvement in the organization are by discussing how you joined the board, what experiences you may have had recently at an on-site visit to the organization or at an event the organization hosted. Talk about some recent accomplishments of the organization that you are especially proud of as a board member. Then, hand the baton to the staff member.

You, the staff member, should provide more "hard-data" about the organization. How many people it has served. Where its funding has come from in the last year. What its specific organizational challenges have been, where its needs are. If you have any specific fundraising initiatives underway, now is a good time to bring them up and describe them. At this point, the board member can jump in at any point to affirm some specific point, tell a story, or ask his or her friend if there are any questions. You'll know if the donor is "with you" if he or she interrupts during your conversation to ask questions. Interested donors always do. If the donor prospect seems distracted, or unusually quiet, you may be competing with his worries and work distractions. Keep your presentation all the more focused if that is the case.

After you have answered questions, the board member can once again express personal enthusiasm for the organization and thank the prospect again for meeting. At this point, the staff member needs to spring into action. The staff member needs to make the ask. This is why the staff member comes along on this meeting. The board member is liable to feel uncomfortable switching gears from "friendly chat" to "money talk," but the staff person can dispassionately ask. The board member might be tempted to change the amount of the ask downward at this point, but the staff person will stick to the script. The staff member will ask for a predetermined amount. It's important to ask for more than you expect to receive given human nature. Everyone is going to try to get away with giving the lowest amount possible, not necessarily from being a cheapskate, but possibly from not wanting to "exert too much." The staff person is there to stretch the donor. The staff person should say something to the effect of: "John, thanks for meeting with us today. Terry and I really appreciate your interest in our organization. That's why we would like to ask you to consider making a gift of $5,000 to support our year-end campaign. Would you be able to make a gift of $5,000?"

HOT TIP

THE STAFF MEMBER TALKS ABOUT DATA AND ASKS FOR THE MONEY

At this time, the board member and the staff person should pretend to be deer caught in headlights. No motion, no comments. The temptation will be great to break the silence and reduce the awkwardness, but everyone needs to shut up. The tension you may feel is good. It means you are letting the donor decide what to do. There are several possible outcomes after the question is out. One is that the donor will say yes. That's the answer you want. Still, if the donor says yes too quickly, it might mean that you have not asked for a high enough amount. If you are stretching the donor, you will probably need to have a little more of a follow-up conversation. If the donor prospect says "I need to think about it," then you have gotten what is probably the most common answer. It's natural for people to want to think about giving away a large amount of money. You should acknowledge that you respect the donor for wanting to do this, but you should also ask how much time the donor needs to think before you follow up. You don't want to leave the meeting without an agreed-upon follow-up strategy. Many a donor is lost that way.

However, the answer you are also quite likely to hear is NO. The old fundraising saw goes that you have to ask three times before you get to the yes. Board and staff need to respond as appropriate, remembering what we said earlier about "dissecting the no." Your organization needs you to know how to do this process and to begin doing it sooner rather than later. There's nothing like the real thing!

Group Role Playing—
When You're Getting Ready for the Real Thing

If it sounds dangerous and scary to just dive right into face-to-face donor solicitation meetings, then take heart! There is something that you can do to minimize the risks—role play! This exercise is a good one to perform on a regular basis, whether your board members are hardened veterans or the greenest novices. By role playing, you move past what should be trivial challenges: knowing what words to use to describe the organization's mission, programs, and current activities; being familiar with facts and figures that might be tongue-twisters if you have never uttered them before; and becoming physically comfortable with sitting in front of someone and looking her in the eye. My advice is to take a good sized chunk of one of your board meetings or to set aside a special Saturday-morning retreat to discuss goals for solicitation for the year and to do some role-playing.

Break up your board into groups of three. In these groups, one person will play the donor prospect, one person will play the board member, and one person will play the staff person who will go along to make the ask. Each role-play should last no more than 10 minutes, so there is an element of pressure to complete the task. Once the ten minutes are up, the team members in each group should rotate roles, so by the time you're done, everyone has had a chance to play each role. Be sure before you begin that you know what the roles of board and staff are. As for the role of donor? Your job is to ask hard questions and make them work to get your money.

HOT TIP

ROLE-PLAYING REDUCES THE RISK OF SOMETHING GOING WRONG IN SOLICITATION

If you are the board member, tell the person playing the prospect who he is and what he is like before your start. The team members playing board and staff need to agree on an amount to ask for before starting. Someone, ideally a staff person for your organization who is not involved in the role-playing, should be the timekeeper for the group exercise. This person will remind you that you have ten minutes to do small talk, state your case, and wrap up the ask. Two minutes before the round ends, the timekeeper should announce a two-minute warning so you can pour on the charm.

After the first round, stay where you are and check in as a group. Discuss what happened and whether there were any surprises or problems. Give a round of applause to any especially skillful or wily solicitors who crack the toughest donors. Then, switch roles and try again.

In some instances, particularly with a donor you have successfully solicited face-to-face in the past, a solicitation letter may take the place of a meeting. First offer the donor the option of getting together in person again, for a report on how his or her gift was used in the past year. Also let him know you're asking for a repeat gift. If the donor is too busy for the meeting, or not interested in using the time that way, tell him that you will be sending a letter instead. Follow up the letter with a phone call to ask if a gift is in the cards.

SAMPLE—SOLICITATION LETTERS

SAMPLE ONE

October 3, 2003

Lara Jones
Jones & Company
99 Osgood Place
Pittsburgh, PA 15207

Dear Lara:

I want to thank you again for your generous support of Ultra Nonprofit in 2002. That support has meant so much to the low-income young women we serve and allowed to us to reach almost 200 young women in the past year.

As you are probably aware, the economy in 2003 has created an extremely challenging funding environment. While Ultra Nonprofit has had to make significant cuts to our budget, we have not reduced our programming or the number of young women we serve in 2003. But, in order to sustain that level of services, we need the support of donors like you. That is why I am writing to ask you for a special gift of $2,000 for Ultra Nonprofit as we head into the final stretch of 2003.

I could provide you with a long list of Ultra Nonprofit's accomplishments since we began in 1998, but to keep it brief, I'll just give you one crucial piece of information: 80% of Ultra Nonprofit's high school graduates are going to college; 26% of these college attendees are going to 4-year schools.

Why is this statistic so extraordinarily high? First, we work with young women consistently over the course of their high school experience. Second, they learn to believe in themselves and develop a sense of competence that they don't get in school. Third, we provide them with academic and college preparatory experience they don't get in school. Fourth, they develop strong relationships with Ultra Nonprofit staff who become role models for their success. Young women who come to Ultra Nonprofit learn to think big and expect something from their lives. We not only give them job and leadership skills; we help them realize their goals.

While Ultra Nonprofit has maintained its high standards and has continued to serve approximately 200 young women in 2003, we have had to do so in spite of a very unfavorable funding climate. The continuing decline of the stock market has caused local foundations to make fewer or no grants this year. This has caused many nonprofit agencies to lay off staff or close their doors. Thankfully, Ultra Nonprofit won't meet with this fate. We've been too fiscally prudent. However, we need your help to stay on track through the end of 2003 and into 2004.

Ultra Nonprofit has kicked off a year-end individual donor campaign with a goal of raising an additional $95,000 in individual contributions between now and December 31, 2003. Thanks to the generosity of three of our top donors, Ultra Nonprofit is starting the campaign with a $20,000 challenge gift. This means that for every dollar contributed between now and December 31, these donors will match that gift dollar for dollar, up to a total of $20,000!

Every personal gift makes a huge difference in our ability to keep our programs strong, serve the same numbers of girls this year and into next year, and maintain the quality standards Ultra Nonprofit is known for.

I am writing to ask if you can make a personal gift of $2,000 to our year-end campaign. If you are able to make this gift in October, it will give some early momentum to our fundraising and can help us raise our first $20,000 to meet the challenge.

I have enclosed a contribution envelope with this letter so you can use it if you decide you would like to participate in our campaign. I'll call you to follow up this letter and look forward to catching up with you!

Yours truly,

Deborah Director
Ultra Nonprofit Executive Director

SAMPLE TWO

February 10, 2004

Harriet Nelson
12841 La Cresta Drive
Santa Fe, NM 75011

Dear Harriet,

I want to begin by thanking you for your very generous support to Ultra Nonprofit last year, including two gifts of stock and your involvement in the BIG EVENT luncheon. We are so grateful for your commitment to making a difference in the lives of low-income young women, and we want you to know that your support makes wonderful things happen!

Because you are one of our most committed supporters, I am writing to invite you to join a very special group of Ultra Nonprofit donors—the donors to Ultra Nonprofit's new "Invest in Her Success" Program.

Individuals who contribute to Invest in Her Success provide a very special gift that will make a lasting, positive impact on a young woman's life.

When you become a donor to Invest in Her Success, you provide the funds to support a young woman's participation through a complete Ultra Nonprofit program or even multiple programs. The young woman benefits by having an experience that will change her life, and you benefit by being personally involved in the process.

I am writing to ask if you and Rich would consider making a gift of $5,000 to Invest in Her Success this spring. A gift at this level covers the cost of putting one young woman through multiple Ultra Nonprofit programs. In exchange for your support, you will receive samples of her work and the materials she's created, plus find out about her progress through high school and college. We would also work to arrange for you to meet the young woman at an Ultra Nonprofit event.

Alternatively, if you would prefer to make a gift of $2,500, this gift would cover one young woman's participation in our Technology and Leadership Program. You would receive samples of all her work and the materials she's created in TLP and find out more about her personal goals.

By contributing at this level, you are investing in an individual young woman.

However, you'll be more than just an investor—you'll also be a hero.

I'll call to follow up and see if you would be interested in helping Ultra Nonprofit and the young women we serve by committing a gift of this level to Invest in Her Success. Your participation will help us launch this program this year and continue to build it throughout 2004.

Thank you for considering our request.

Sincerely,

Director of Development Nelson
Ultra Nonprofit Dirctor of Development

Following up Your Solicitation Meeting

If your donor has said, "I need to think about it," in your solicitation meeting, and you have negotiated a date for your follow-up, be sure to stick to the agreed upon schedule. Doing so will show the donor that you are serious about the request and that you intend to pursue it, in a friendly way. Ideally, the board member will be the person to call or email to check back in. If the donor had requested additional information to help her make her decision, then the staff person should have jumped right on it as soon as the meeting was over. By the time the board member makes contact, the donor prospect should be equipped to make a decision. If the donor decides that the time isn't right to make the gift, thank her nonetheless for thinking over the request, and let her know that you would like to ask again later in the year, when things may be in better alignment for a gift. If the donor says yes, respond with a hearty and enthusiastic thank-you, and ask about how she would like to make the gift. Instruct her about how to make out the check, where to send it. Offer to have the staff member call to get a credit card number. If the donor wants to make a gift of stock, follow up with transfer instructions. Make it easy for the newly convinced donor.

TROPHY CASE

There was a couple who had been giving $1,000 annually to Good Charity. However, I knew they contributed millions of dollars annually to many other local organizations. Obviously, Good Charity needed to ask them for a bigger gift. I asked an advisory board member who's a close friend of the couple to set up a meeting where we asked the donors to give $29,000 for an international medical trip to a specific country. The donors said they would consider, but also asked us to send additional details to help them decide. Two days later, we received word that they had decided to focus on local giving instead of funding our work—although the cause was worthy. Despite receiving a "no," I went ahead and mailed them the details they had requested at our meeting. After reading my letter describing specific tragic medical cases Good Charity deals with in this country, they called to say they would give the $29,000 for our work.

A simple way to make sure your donor doesn't forget about making the gift is to send a letter reminding him about the pledge. The following letter is an example of what you can say. Notice that the letter includes a remit envelope to make it extra easy for the donor to respond with a check or credit card number.

SAMPLE—SOLICITATION FOLLOW UP LETTER

October 1, 2003

Lawrence Jones
1661 Terrace Road
Palo Alto, CA 94306

Dear Mr. Jones:

Thank you so much for your pledge of $1,000 to Ultra Nonprofit! Jamie Boardmember has filled me in on your contribution and has asked me to send you the enclosed contribution envelope for your convenience. The envelope is addressed and stamped for your use.

I want you to know that we appreciate your support very much and that it could not come at a better time since this year has been a particularly challenging one due to the lagging economy and a general downturn in foundation gifts. Your contribution will be put to good use serving low-income young women in Ultra Nonprofit's programs.

We look forward to staying in touch with you about how your gift has made a difference!

Sincerely,

Director of Development Nelson
Ultra Nonprofit Director of Development

Encl: contribution envelope

A T THE beginning of this book, we mentioned the challenge gift as one of the essential components for the well-developed individual giving program. In this chapter, we will show you some examples of how to ask for a challenge gift and how to describe how it works to your donors. While the challenge gift is something you could work without, if you had to, it's something you really want to go all out to secure, because it will make your work much, much easier later. A challenge gift is like a lever—it gives you the power to lift up other gifts without so much exertion. In fact, what the challenge gift is doing is providing "leverage," that magical term people use in the financial world to describe something that lets you make more money with less effort. Once you've tried a challenge gift, you are not going to want to work without one ever again.

A challenge gift works by providing confidence, incentive, and urgency.

The confidence comes from seeing someone else—the person (or the foundation) providing the challenge gift—who is willing to put himself on the line by committing an amount of money, often a large amount, to this organization's cause.

The incentive comes from the "match," the function of the challenge gift in matching other contributions that are given, dollar for dollar, up to the amount of the challenge itself.

Additionally, because a challenge gift also comes with a deadline, it provides a sense of urgency, because donors will have only a short, set time to respond to the challenge and earn their match for the organization.

HOT TIP

A CHALLENGE GIFT PROVIDES CONFIDENCE, INCENTIVE, AND URGENCY

So how well do campaigns with challenges work? Usually, they work extremely well, so long as you have set them up to include a challenge gift that is of sufficient size to generate excitement but not so big that your donor pool cannot possibly contribute enough to earn the match. You will know you are selecting a reasonable amount if you start with the amount of the challenge gift, then count up the number of solicitations you plan to make as part of the campaign, and how much money you expect to receive, then add in a figure for gifts coming from direct mail, based either on how you have done in the past with direct mail, or based on an estimate of how many people will send a gift, and what you believe the average sized gift will be. This will give you a good ballpark total for the campaign. Oftentimes, in fact, a challenge can end up earning more money than an equivalent match. Sometimes, you can raise more than you would ever have imagined.

You can secure your challenge from an individual donor, or you can secure it from a foundation. Sometimes, you may need to combine challenge gifts together to have a sufficiently large sum to stimulate real interest.

On the following pages are some examples of how to ask a major donor or a foundation for a challenge gift. Following these examples is a direct mail letter showing you how to incorporate the challenge into your appeal.

TROPHY CASE

One year, I decided we needed a large matching gift to help Our Org reach its annual goal. I had been cultivating a donor who had given $10,000 per year up to that point, and I knew the time was right to get him more involved. I asked the donor if he would pledge a $50,000 challenge gift that Our Org would then work to match with an additional $50,000. He agreed. With the help of this challenge gift, which was included in a direct mail appeal to 9,000 donors and potential donors, Good Charity was able to raise not just an additional $50,000, but rather a whopping $112,000 in additional gifts in the timeframe specified. Needless to say, we called that campaign a success.

ASKING A MAJOR DONOR FOR A CHALLENGE GIFT

SAMPLE ONE

August 1, 2003

Doug Smith
1 Sea View Street
Portland, OR 98611

Dear Doug:

I want to thank you again for your generous donation of $5,000 to Ultra
Nonprofit in 2002. That support has meant so much to the low-income
young women we serve and allowed to us to reach almost 200 young
women. As you know, the economy has created an extremely challenging
funding environment. While Ultra Nonprofit has had to make significant
cuts to our budget, we have not reduced our programming or the number
of young women we serve in 2003. But, in order to sustain that level of services, we need the support of donors like you. That is why I am writing to
ask you for a special $10,000 challenge gift for Ultra Nonprofit as we head
into the second half of 2003.

I could provide you with a long list of Ultra Nonprofit's accomplishments
since we began in 1998, but to keep it brief, I'll just give you one crucial piece
of information: 86% of Ultra Nonprofit's high school graduates are going to
college; 26% of these college attendees are going to 4-year schools.

Why is this statistic so extraordinarily high? First, we work with young women
consistently over the course of their high school experience. Second, they
learn to believe in themselves and develop a sense of competence that they
don't get in school. Third, we provide them with academic and college preparatory experience they don't get in school. Fourth, they develop strong
relationships with Ultra Nonprofit staff who become role models for their
success. Young women who come to Ultra Nonprofit learn to think big and
expect something from their lives. We not only give them job and leadership
skills, we help them realize their goals.

To forestall further cuts and sustain our service to girls at the same level,
we are looking to use a challenge gift to launch an individual donor cam-

paign lasting from September 1 through the end of December 2003. This campaign—which will be the single focus of Ultra Nonprofit's outreach and fundraising through the remainder of the year—would raise critical funds to sustain our programming at current levels during this tough economic time. Specifically, we propose to use a $30,000 challenge as a vehicle to raise additional funding in the amount of $130,000 by citing it in every fundraising effort through the end of 2003.

By providing a challenge gift of $10,000 toward the total $30,000 challenge, you would give Ultra Nonprofit the ability to leverage all of our fundraising efforts this fall. In the world of nonprofit fundraising, this kind of challenge consistently produces results—the incentive and the urgency of the challenge encourage donors to give generously and give early.

We at Ultra Nonprofit have so appreciated your gifts in years past and I hope you are able to continue this support. I will call you in a week or two to see if this is possible.

Thanks in advance for your time and consideration.

Sincerely

Deborah Director
Executive Director

ASKING A FOUNDATION FOR A CHALLENGE GIFT

September 8, 2003

Diane Jones
Program Officer, Community Health
The Big Foundation
225 Clinton Street, 5th Floor
Melbourne, CA 90025

Dear Ms. Jones,

I am submitting this letter of intent to the Big Foundation for consideration for a grant of $25,000 to be used as part of a $50,000 challenge that will help leverage $150,000 in additional funds in our 2004 annual individual donor campaign.

Ultra Nonprofit appreciates the foundation's consideration of our request, and we hope to be invited to submit a full proposal.

Sincerely,

Deborah Director
Ultra Nonprofit Executive Director

PROPOSAL # C-2004-0017

September 8, 2003

Diane Jones
Program Officer, Community Health
The Big Foundation
225 Clinton Street, 5th Floor
Melbourne, CA 90025

Dear Ms. Jones,

I am submitting this letter of intent to the Big Foundation for consideration for a challenge grant of $25,000 to $50,000 which will be used to
leverage $150,000 in additional funds in our 2004 annual individual donor
campaign.

Ultra Nonprofit's mission is to provide meaningful employment and leadership opportunities for low-income young women, ages 14–18. We hire them
to create media and education projects that express their own voices and
experiences. Ultra Nonprofit equips young women with the life, leadership,
and job skills they need to succeed.

Ultra Nonprofit was founded in 1998 and became an independent 501c3
in 1999. Since our inception we have successfully implemented four programs, have served over 250 young women, and have grown from a staff
of two employees to a full-time staff of 10. Ultra Nonprofit has been and
remains capable of supporting the proposed program and meeting our
budgetary needs. Since 1999, our annual budget has grown from under
$200,000 to almost $1,000,000 per year. Not only have we been able to
raise funds to meet our budget, we have used those funds to grow the
organization wisely.

Ultra Nonprofit serves urban, low-income young women between the ages
of 14 and 18. Ethnically, the young women we serve represent the diversity
of San Francisco's low-income population: 48% are Latina, 35% African-
American, 13% Asian/Pacific-Islander, and 4% are White. It is important to
emphasize that in recruiting for all our programs, Ultra Nonprofit serves
young women that others agencies cannot accommodate: women who are
pregnant or parenting, living in shelter, or otherwise precariously housed.
Our program participants are primarily from low-income neighborhoods in

San Francisco. Many of the young women are multi-lingual English speakers with varying levels of literacy.

Low-income young women traditionally lack meaningful economic and professional opportunities that allow them to envision a positive, productive future for themselves, as well as the job skills and education that would allow them to ultimately access higher paying jobs. Nowhere is this more true than in San Francisco's Mission, Fillmore, Western Addition, and Bayview/Hunter's Point districts - neighborhoods where the majority of our participants live - where almost 40% of households live in poverty and less than 15% complete college (2000 Census). Furthermore, with unemployment much higher in these neighborhoods than in the county as a whole, our participants have few professional role models, and with poverty so high, even less experience with technology and computers, which is essential for them to compete in the job market.

In order to effectively serve low-income young women, we feel it is critical to provide long-term, time-intensive services in a safe, girl-friendly environment, where participants form long-lasting relationships with staff members who become their role models for success. In that regard, it is crucial that our programs serve low-income young women over time, and we hire participants as interns or staff members beyond their initial employment opportunity.

Ultra Nonprofit current programming includes:

- The Tech Program provides paid technology, life, leadership, and job skills training to 72 low-income young women per year.
- The Community Program hires 48 young women a year to develop leadership and activism skills and participate in community service projects of their own choosing.
- The Media Program pays 30 young women a year to develop and hone their speaking skills and use these skills to address young women's issues across the Bay Area and beyond.
- The College Bound Program provides career, college, and life-planning services to all Ultra Nonprofit participants via workshops, individual college counseling and homework assistance, college visits, SAT classes, and participation in an Individual Development Account Program. Thanks to the College Bound program, 86% of Ultra Nonprofit's high school graduates are going to college; 26% of these college attendees are going to 4-year schools.

Some of the goals addressed by Ultra Nonprofit's work include:

- Increasing access to and availability of youth development and youth leadership programs.

- Increasing access to sustainable livelihoods through workforce development, economic development, and assistance, particularly to young women.

- Increasing youth civic participation and leadership.

Ultra Nonprofit experienced serious fundraising challenges during the difficult economic climate of 2003 and had to implement strategic cuts to our budget. In 2004, we are looking to use a challenge grant to launch a special individual donor campaign lasting from January through the end of December 2004. This campaign—which will be the single focus of Ultra Nonprofit's outreach and fundraising through the year—would raise critical funds to sustain our programming at current levels during this tough economic time.

Specifically, we propose to use a $50,000 challenge as a vehicle to raise additional funding in the amount of $150,000 by citing it in every fundraising effort throughout 2003. These include:

- Direct mail to our donor database of 5,000 individual recipients;

- Six private house parties with over 100 guests in attendance;

- Face-to-face donor solicitation meetings with our 40 to 50 biggest donors;

- The BIG EVENT Awards Luncheon which typically hosts an audience of 700;

- Ultra Nonprofit newsletter which circulates to over 5,000 individuals;

- An email bulletin that goes to 500 individual recipients;

- The Ultra Nonprofit website which has over 9,000 discrete individual visitors each month;

- Press stories about Ultra Nonprofit (in October 2002, the San Francisco Chronicle ran a two-page story with photos about Ultra Nonprofit, which was the cover of the Bay Area section; we are now planning a major press effort that would support this year-end campaign by gaining similar coverage);

- Additional personal outreach efforts of our Board of Directors and Advisory Board.

A challenge grant from the Big Foundation would give Ultra Nonprofit the ability to leverage all of our fundraising efforts this fall. In our experience, this kind of challenge consistently produces results—the incentive and the urgency of the challenge encourage donors to give generously and give early. Without a challenge to work off of, we are concerned that Ultra Nonprofit will have a much harder time reaching our overall fundraising goal. We hope to partner with a local foundation such as the Big Foundation which values the empowerment of low-income young women and wants to help organizations serving these young women at a tough economic time.

In addition to making this request of the Big Foundation, Ultra Nonprofit is also approaching other foundations that currently support us, as well as past and current individual funders, to inquire about this type of gift. If we do not receive one gift in the amount we are seeking, we can also combine two or more smaller gifts to reach our goal. As is typical with this sort of campaign, the challenge gift would not be paid out until Ultra Nonprofit has completed its fundraising goal.

For 2004, Ultra Nonprofit's budget is $850,000.

The year 2003 proved a very difficult year for fundraising and 2004 should be similarly problematic, but Ultra Nonprofit is approaching this challenge with enthusiasm and creativity. We would be thrilled to have the Big Foundation join us as a partner in this campaign.

Thank you very much for considering this letter of inquiry.

Sincerely,

Deborah Director
Ultra Nonprofit Executive

CHAPTER NINE—
THE CAMPAIGN

CAMPAIGN is a structured effort, defined by a dollar goal, a deadline, a specific need, and oftentimes a donor incentive, to raise money for an organization. I suggest you define all of your individual donor fundraising in terms of the campaign. You will have an annual campaign for the year, but you can also have smaller campaigns that feed into this larger campaign, such as a spring campaign, a fall campaign—pretty much any campaign you can define that will help you reach your goal.

The campaign is where all the elements of your carefully crafted and developed individual giving program come together to create a harmonious whole. Your direct mail, events, donor communications, giving tiers and benefits, your major donor relationships, your board members' involvement all come together to define how successful you will be.

The campaign is the crowning feature of your well developed individual giving program. Once you have become equipped and organized enough to launch one of these babies, you will have gained the control needed to direct donor giving around your calendar and program needs.

Some people think of a campaign as something elaborate and intensive that is reserved for large organizations raising millions of dollars to build a new museum, construct a new animal shelter, or buy a new office building. It's true that efforts like these—called "bricks and mortar" campaigns— are among the biggest and most elaborate examples of campaigns, however, that doesn't mean you aren't allowed to use a campaign if you aren't building a structure. A campaign can simply mean, "We need to raise $100,000 more in individual gifts by December 30 in order to deliver the same level of service to our clients at the beginning of next year." Don't let anybody tell you this tool is too advanced for your young organization. Just do it!

This is the basic breakdown of the steps involved in defining and launching a campaign.

1) Define the need for the money you are going to raise.

2) Get a sense of the amount of money required to cover this need.

3) Determine the deadline for raising this money.

4) Identify who may be a challenge donor for the campaign and how much she can give.

5) Determine if you need to also approach a foundation or additional individuals to combine their gifts.

6) Calculate how many solicitations you will make, of which donors, and for how much money.

7) Determine what kind of mail appeal you will incorporate into the campaign and how many donors and prospects it will be mailed to.

8) Determine other components that will contribute to the campaign, such as house parties, corporate matching, car donations, etc.

9) Brief your board on the campaign details and get their buy-in before you start.

10) Write some language that everyone who will be in-

volved in raising money for the campaign can use to help them solicit gifts.

11) Approach your prospective challenge gifts donor or donors and secure their commitment.

12) Announce the campaign and the challenge in your newsletter and on your website.

13) Begin soliciting major gifts toward the campaign goal.

14) Keep your supporters informed of your progress through your newsletter, your website, and letters updating them.

15) When you get close to your goal, return to those who gave early gifts and see if they will give a little more to help you get to the finish line.

16) Announce your achievement of the goal and thank everyone who gave.

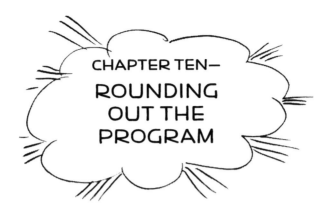

CHAPTER TEN—
ROUNDING OUT THE PROGRAM

HERE are some other components you can add to your individual donor program over time to maximize its potential. This list is by no means the whole universe of individual giving bells and whistles. I'm confident that your creativity will produce even more additions to your program. Try something out and see if it works. If it doesn't, try something else!

• Car donations

People who may not have the means to write you a check of any amount may still be sitting on something that can convert to a cash donation—a used car. Car donation programs are myriad. You have certainly seen the billboard advertisements lining the freeway and heard the ubiquitous radio ads about various car donation programs. These programs either exist as independent entities or work directly through a nonprofit organization. The independent entities accept donated cars, take a fee, often high, and then give the remainder to a charity of the donor's choice. A better option for donors is usually a car donation program that is set up through the nonprofit itself. You can set up this type of program by finding a car auction house that is willing to accept donations on your behalf, process and sell the cars, take a fee you negotiate in advance, and return the rest to you. Make this option available to your donors. Keep in mind that recent changes to charitable-giving laws have reduced the amount donors can claim for this type of donation.

- **Gifts of stock**

You need to get set up for this type of gift by establishing a relationship with a stock brokerage and setting up an account to receive gifts of stock. Donors often want to make a gift of stock to avoid paying capital gains taxes on appreciated stock. By giving the appreciated shares to you, the nonprofit organization, the donor avoids the tax AND gets to write off the donation on her taxes. You get the money from the sale of the stock. It really is a win-win situation.

SAMPLE—LANGUAGE ABOUT GIFT OF STOCK

When you would like to make a gift of stock to our nonprofit, here are few steps to follow:

Notification of Donor Intent

Regardless of the method chosen to deliver a gift of stock, the donor or the transferring broker must provide the following information, for audit and acknowledgment purposes:

* Donor's name and complete address
* Name and number of securities transferred
* Broker's name and phone number
* Approximate dollar value of gift

You may provide a letter, or send an e-mail to communicate this information at time of transfer to:

Name of Organization
Attn: Director of Development
Address
City, State Zip
E-mail: development@organization.org
Phone: 415-555-8880 x303
Fax: 415-555-8884

Securities Delivered Electronically

The following information will enable your broker to facilitate an electronic transfer of stock:

Brokerage: Name of Brokerage
Address
City, State, Zip
DTC Number: Number here
Account Number: Account number here
Account Name: Name of organization
(Tax ID: I.D. here)
Phone: Phone here
Fax: Fax here
Attn: Agent's name here

- **Planned giving**

Planned giving is a way for donors to include your non-profit organization in their estate-planning so they can give you a gift when they die. Sounds gruesome? It's really not. It's another way you can make donors feel good about giving, in this case, because they know they can continue to make a difference in this world even when they've passed on. Planned giving programs are usually something that large, established nonprofits set up, especially organizations with older donor bases, including people who have substantial wealth to manage and who are old enough to be thinking about what will happen to their wealth when they die. However, if your younger, developing nonprofit thinks about planned giving now and incorporates some aspects of this kind of program into your plans now, you will get a jump on your competition. Donors who make small gifts year in and year out might be sitting on large piles of non-liquid assets, and they might just consider including you in their estate planning if you let them know this option exists.

TROPHY CASE

There was a donor who contributed $50 annually to a nonprofit I worked for. He was an orphan who'd never married nor had any children. He found out about our organization when the executive director went to speak at his local club. Every year, he received the same cultivation as every other donor giving at his level. However, we quietly promoted planned giving through our regular printed materials and website. The man lived to be 94 years old. When he died, he left $600,000 to our organization in his will.

Bequests (leaving money in a will) are just one way donors can leave a gift upon their death. The other vehicles for planned giving are various and somewhat beyond the scope of this book. I suggest calling up some of your local, large, institutional nonprofits to ask them to send you samples of their planned giving materials to look at. Or, go on their websites to see how they discuss the topic. You can begin by mentioning the words "consider including Our Nonprofit in your estate planning" on your brochures, remit envelopes, newsletters, and other materials that you share with your donors. Include information about planned giving on your website. Ask your board members to consider including your nonprofit in their plans, too.

If you are seriously considering starting to promote the idea of planned giving—and I hope you are—then consult an attorney who specializes in this area to advise you and your donors.

- **Escrip**

There are myriad rebate programs designed to support schools and nonprofit organizations. One of the best known of these is the eScrip Program. Most people find eScrip to be pretty simple and convenient. All you do is register your grocery club card and your debit/credit cards with eScrip. When you shop, participating eScrip merchants track your purchases. At the end of each month, the merchants provide a rebate to eScrip, which deposits the money you've earned for your designated nonprofit—just by shopping as you always do—directly into the nonprofit's bank account. There is the potential for your organization to raise a substantial number of dollars from rebates if enough of your donors sign up for the program, but getting them to sign up will require lots of initiative and marketing on your part. Still, you may find the pay-offs worthwhile. Another similar program is Schoolpop, which brings together store, catalog and online merchants with the community to raise money for youth organizations.

- **Online giving**

In this day and age, your nonprofit really can't operate without having a website. In fact, I'm guessing that you already have the website. However, have you set it up so your donors can make a gift online? By making it convenient for your donors to pull a credit card out of a wallet and make that gift, you capture "impulse" gifts that someone who is busy and can't find an envelope and a stamp won't make. Also, the technology has improved substantially to allow you to assure your donors that their personal information will be secure and confidential on your site. Make sure you use a secure server with anti-theft capabilities to protect your donors.

- **Corporate matching gifts**

An easy way to increase the impact of your donation is to have your employer match it. Thousands of companies have matching gift programs that will double or even triple, individual tax-deductible contributions made by their employees. Check with your personnel office to find out about your company's program. They will give you a matching gift form that you can fill out and send in with your contribution.

- **Phone banking**

This is a technique you can combine with direct mail to great effect. Gather your board and volunteers on one evening at a location where you have enough phone lines so each person can man a phone. If you don't have a place like this, see if you can find a local bank or investment company that would be willing to donate their space and phones for your use. Give everyone a script to read from and have them call the donors and prospects who have received your direct mail. By combining phone calls with the letter, you increase your chances of receiving more gifts. If anyone who receives the call requests that you not call in the future, make a note and add this to your database. Send remit envelopes to any people who are called who say they have lost their original remit.

SAMPLE—PHONE SCRIPT

Hi, this is _____ from the Ultra Nonprofit board of directors calling for _____. I'm calling on behalf of _____ _____ who is also on our board.

I'm calling because we recently sent you an appeal letter for our year-end campaign to raise an additional $75,000 by December 31.

I wanted to call to share the good news that we have raised $46,000 toward the goal. That means we still have $29,000 to raise in the next few weeks.

Did you receive a copy of the letter?

Yes, Received Letter—did you have a chance to read it?

Have you already sent a gift?
Thank you for helping us get this far toward our goal!

No, Did not Receive Letter—I'll mail you another copy.
Check that address is correct.

Would you be willing to send a contribution to help us reach our goal? A gift of any amount will help. Gifts of $250 and above get a free copy of our new book published by Full Speed Press.

Yes?—I'll send you an envelope to use for your gift.

You can also pay by credit card over the phone.
(Take information on sheet)

No? Can't send a gift right now?—thanks for taking the time to talk.

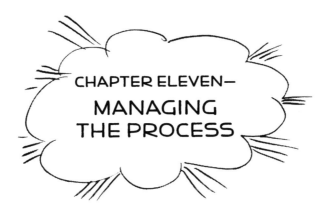

CHAPTER ELEVEN—
MANAGING THE PROCESS

A S I mentioned in the first chapter of this book, you need to have a written development plan if you want to be successful in raising individual donor dollars. Below is an example of what a basic development plan looks like. Be prepared to review your plan several times during the year and make changes and adjustments wherever you need to. This kind of plan is supposed to be a guide, not a straightjacket!

SAMPLE DEVELOPMENT PLAN

Our Org Draft Fundraising Plan
12/9/01

Basic Components of This Plan:
o   Board development as #1 priority

o   Leveraged fundraising campaign building off of board gift and including lead individual and lead foundation gifts

o   Basic regular membership and basic major donor work

o   Foundation work—identifying prospects and writing the boilerplate grant proposal

o   Plan for developing the basic fundraising tools and materials o   One basic fundraising event that can grow over time

o   House parties hosted by board members or other supporters

o   Development of general infrastructure that will support any and all
    fundraising activities into the future

Task Timeline

In parentheses, we indicate which component of the fundraising program
the action relates to.

January 2002

- (Board) Draft recruitment letter and create packet for potential new
  board members

- (Direct Mail) Put all of board and advisory board prospects in the database and include them in general direct mail appeals.

- (Major Donors) Call to set up face-to-face visits with key donors for
  large gifts

- (Board) Identify potential new board members; recommend reaching 7
  to 10 total

- (Campaign) Determine total goal for annual campaign ($20,000,
  $30,000)

- (Events) Call contact about raffling box at Giants game.

- (Foundation) Call foundations to gather their guidelines

- (Foundation) Review guidelines and select those Our Org is eligi-
  ble for

- (General) Explore new arrangement for stock gifts.

- (Other) % of sales day—get businesses where Our Org has connections
  to donate a percentage of sales on a special day to Our Org.

- (Other) Car donations—encourage donors to consider donating their
  old cars to Our Org; can set up relationship with car auction house easily.
  Need to promote idea to donors.

- (Other) eScrip—ask all board, advisory committee members, and
  other supporters to sign up; their purchases will support Our Org
  each month.

February 2002

- (Board) Begin approaching potential new board members

- (Corporate) Corporate matching—ask donors to inquire about corporate matching by their employers; include information about this type of program in Our Org newsletter and provide list of some large employers who have this kind of program.

- (Foundation) Hire professional grant writer to create boilerplate proposal and LOI

- (General) Recruit more office and general volunteers

- (Major Donors) Talk to board members about their donors and see who has major donor potential and determine best strategy for soliciting

- (Other) Brainstorm potential fee-for-service/earned income activities Our Org can do. Speaking engagements? Sell curriculum? Training and classes for fee?

March 2002

- (Board) Recruit potential new board members

- (Board/Campaign) Ask board members for personal board gifts

- (Direct Mail) Plan for next newsletter; set the schedule for mailing

- (Foundation) Complete boilerplate proposal and LOI covering all programs

- (Foundation) Record foundation deadlines for proposals or letters on a calendar

- (General) Recruit more office and general volunteers

- (Major Gifts) Make list of potential individual donors who could give $100 or more

April 2002

- (Board) Continue approaching potential new board members

- (Direct Mail) Write content of newsletter, print, and mail; use the newsletter to promote eScrip, car donations, corporate matching, and other fundraising-related topics

- (Event) Conduct raffle for Giants box

- (Foundation) Calls to key foundations to inquire about what type of proposal to send.

- (Foundation) Creating tracking sheet for proposals, replies, and reports.

- (Foundations) Submit applications to foundations and follow up.

- (General) Secure letters of support from friends of Our Org.

- (Major Donors) Call to set up face-to-face visits with key donors for large gifts

May 2002

- (Board) Continue approaching potential new board members

- (Direct Mail) Print and mail appeal letter to general membership; use the annual campaign as the trigger for the request, giving a sense of focus and urgency

- (Foundations) Submit applications to other foundations and follow up on submissions.

- (Foundations) Update foundation tracking sheet

- (Foundation) Make multiple copies of foundation support materials

- (General) Recruit more office and general volunteers

- (Individual Donors) Meet with advisory board members about individual prospects

- (Major Donors) Call to set up face-to-face visits with key donors for large gifts

June 2002

- (Board) Continue approaching potential new board members

- (Direct Mail) Phone banking to follow up appeal letter

- (Foundations) Submit applications to other foundations and follow up on submissions.

- (Foundations) Update foundation tracking sheet

- (General) Review fundraising plan and make any necessary adjustments

- (Major Donors) Call to set up face-to-face visits with key donors for large gifts

July 2002

- (Board) Continue approaching potential new board members

- (Event) Begin planning to inaugurate an annual award program for July 2003

- (Foundations) Submit applications to other foundations and follow up submissions

- (Individual Donors/Board) Meet with new board members to discuss their prospects

- (Major Donors) Call to set up face-to-face visits with key donors for large gifts

August 2002

- (Board) Continue approaching potential new board members

- (Campaign) Either announce completion of campaign, or make additional solicitations in order to reach your goal

- (Corporate) Compile list of potential corporate funders from board and advisory leads

- (Events) Secure host and location for 2003 dinner

- (Foundations) Submit applications to other foundations and follow up on submissions

- (Foundations) Update foundation tracking sheet

- (Individual Donors/Board) Add new prospects from new board members to database

September 2002

- (Board) Continue approaching potential new board members

- (Corporate) Send Our Org packets to corporations from list and make follow-up calls

- (Events) Host Our Org evening at the home of board member; 10 to 20 friends invited; host provides food and drink; Our Org staff and host make direct appeal

- (Direct Mail) Plan for next newsletter; set the schedule for mailing
- (Foundations) Submit applications to other foundations and follow up on submissions
- (General) Recruit more office and general volunteers

October 2002

- (Board) Continue approaching potential new board members
- (Direct Mail) Write content of newsletter, print, and mail; use to promote fundraising
- (Foundations) Submit applications to other foundations and follow up on submissions
- (Foundations) Update foundation tracking sheet
- (General) Investigate creating 5-minute video to introduce major donors to Our Org
- (General) Recruit more office and general volunteers

November 2002

- (Board) Continue approaching potential new board members
- (Direct Mail) Clean up database in preparation for year-end mailing
- (Direct Mail) Draft year-end appeal letter, print, and mail.
- (Foundations) Submit applications to other foundations and follow up on submissions
- (General) Recruit more office and general volunteers

December 2002

- (Direct Mail) Write year-end appeal letter and send to all current donors and new prospects suggested by board and advisory members; have board and advisory members sign letters to their prospects.
- (Board) Continue approaching potential new board members
- (Campaign) Create strategy for new annual campaign in 2003
- (Direct Mail) Mail year-end appeal letter
- (Foundations) Follow-up on any outstanding requests

* (General) Revise annual fundraising plan

Appendices

* List of standard support materials to have ready for foundation proposals (attached)

* List of potential foundation funders and their contact information; evaluation of top foundation prospects and their guidelines (below, guidelines attached)

* List of potential individual donors and their contact information (below, contact information attached)

* Hardcopy of donor profile sheet (attached)

* Hardcopy of foundation tracking document (attached)

* Hardcopy of foundation invoice and reporting document (attached)

* Case statement for Our Org to use as basis for direct mail, donor solicitations, and proposals (below)

* Current Funders

* Potential Prospects (Need to Be Contacted for Guidelines)

* Potential Individual Funders for Our Org

* New Individual Prospects and Contact Person

* Organizations to Network With

Case Statement

What is Our Organization?

Our organization is a new nonprofit whose mission is to improve the fairness, accuracy and diversity of news reporting on disability. We do this by developing tools to help journalists and educators examine the complexity of disability issues from differing perspectives.

Our Organization operates from an impartial position that avoids blame or criticism. Instead, Our Organization fosters open, diverse and inclusive dialogue on disability issues. We believe that our society's predominant views on disability are rooted in fear and a lack of awareness. Through a slow, dedicated process, Our Organization intends to raise the awareness of journalists and educators in order to revolutionize news reporting on disability issues. By reshaping journalism to reflect the reality of disability in America, we hope to produce broad and long-lasting changes in society itself.

How did Our Organization start?

As a freelance photographer working primarily in disability communities, Suzie Brown noticed the narrow range of disability perspectives represented in print and electronic news. To expand coverage, she founded Disability Action, which was incorporated in the state of California in June of 1998 and which eventually became Our Organization.

Our Organization received nonprofit status in February 1999. That summer an advisory group formed that focused on how journalists report on disability and how the organization could work with the news industry. In March 2000 the organization committed to being an impartial, independent journalism organization dedicated to educating journalists, educators and students about disability issues. In November 2000 the organization's name changed to Our Organization to more accurately reflect its mission. Our Organization then moved into shared office space at San Francisco College with professors who support its concerns. An interim board of directors formed to complete Our Organization's business plan and oversee the development of the board, which will be expanded in early 2002.

What needs does Our Organization serve?

Much like issues surrounding race, gender and social class, disability is complex rather than monolithic. To produce balanced coverage and a representative picture of constituent groups in society, reporters should be familiar with the controversies and debates among disability communities. To avoid stereotyping, journalists should take into consideration the range of values and aspirations of these groups. In particular, Our Organization is concerned with investigative reporting producing in-depth stories rather than "human-interest" PR pieces. In-depth news stories have the greatest potential either to reinforce or to explode prevailing social stereotypes about disability and to influence policies and attitudes.

Disability studies programs are emerging on university campuses across the United States and abroad to explore the complexity of disability. Scholars and others have identified different models to describe the ways that people with disabilities view themselves and are viewed by others. The Social, Civil Rights, Medical and Independent Living models of disability are examples. Understanding these and other models will enhance reporting on the ways disability intersects with policy, human rights, health-care, technology, business and more. In the meantime, news reporters are missing important information about disability that affects the lives and self-determination of nearly 54 million people with disabilities, the general public and public policy.

Who does Our Organization serve?

As with diversity issues, society's prevailing views on disability also influence journalists and educators who are products of this society. They bring cultural assumptions to their reporting and to their teaching. Our Organization provides the tools that shift the awareness of these individuals. We believe their intentions are good. As they become more aware, invariably they want to learn more.

Our Organization's vision also includes indirect beneficiaries of our work. News influences the public, and, by influencing the public, it also shapes public policies. These policies in turn affect entire communities as well as the quality of life of all who live in them. Through Our Organization's work to foster more accurate and inclusive news reporting, the general public benefits in time from the development of a more humane and enlightened society.

What programs does Our Organization sponsor?

Our Organization's top priority is developing and distributing educational materials for journalists and educators to use in college and university classrooms. These resources include:

- **Classroom curriculum**

  Our Organization director Suzie tests written curriculum in actual college classrooms. In the future, Our Organization will use the curriculum to conduct teacher training at colleges, universities, and journalism schools. Our Organization is focusing now on the creation of a written plan to shape the development of this curriculum.

- **Newsletters**

  Our Organization News is filled with disability-reporting information including examples, do's and don'ts, as well as language tips. It is sent to individuals on our mailing list and is also available on the Our Organization website (www.OurOrganization.org).

- **A Disability-Centric Style Guide**

  The Our Organization Style Guide, now in a test phase on the Our Organization website, will provide journalists with a greater understanding of the appropriate language to use in coverage of disability-related stories. We intend to host monthly conference calls with national disability experts from a variety of fields to continually update the style guide.

- **An Expert Source Database.**

  Our Organization is compiling a database of people who have specific knowledge and understanding of many aspects of disability issues who will be sources journalists can interview for more balanced coverage in their stories.

- **Website**

  Our Organization website provides content and links that offer access to disability-related sources. The website is a means to deliver Our Organization's programs to the broadest range of people possible. Our Organization needs a professional website manager to work on the site and keep it up to date.

In addition, Our Organization is developing an internship program that will enable students to get hands-on experience in disability reporting.

Lastly, Our Organization also collaborates with other diversity efforts and professional journalism organizations to integrate disability into their awareness campaigns. In time, we also want to work toward an expanded diversity statement on accreditation at schools to include appropriate language on disability.

All of these programs will continue to grow with time, staff and funding.

Who else does this kind of work?

In March 2000, Our Organization made the commitment to become the only impartial, independent journalism organization dedicated to addressing the complexity of disability issues. We found that while similar ethnic journalism organizations were making contributions to the field, only outside groups and individuals funded to promote singular views of disability were addressing disability issues. Even in the short time that Our Organization has been in existence, we have found an increasing number of journalists, news organizations and people with disabilities who also recognize the critical need for educational assistance. Outside of Our Organization's efforts, however, there are no systematic, organized attempts to bring disability into the diversity field of journalism.

Where does Our Organization stand in its development?

Despite its short history and status as a start-up nonprofit organization, Our Organization has already reached several important milestones in its development. Our Organization has a passionate executive director, a committed board of directors, and an eminent group of advisory board members from across the country. The organization has been granted 501(c)3 nonprofit status from the Federal government and has put in place financial management systems, donor data management tools, and a fundraising plan. In its first two years of operation, Our Organization has also:

- Built working relationships with San Francisco College and other schools
- Established ties with individual journalists, educators and students across the country,
- Hired a consultant to help us develop our organization,
- Produced and distributed our first newsletter,
- Delivered guest lectures on college campuses, and
- Published our own journalistic pieces and secured media coverage of our organization.

In a relatively short period of time, Our Organization has laid the groundwork for organizational success. This year, the organization must put additional resources in place in order to take significant steps toward developing its programs and fulfilling its mission.

What does Our Organization need in order to grow?

Our Organization's independent, impartial status shapes the organization's funding policy. Funds from sources that advocate a specific disability perspective or that highlight one perspective over another are not accepted. In addition, corporate and government contributions are reviewed on a case-by-case basis.

Given these self-imposed fundraising restrictions, it is imperative that Our Organization develop a strong individual donor base and also pursue all potential sources of foundation funding. Our Organization already has a fund development plan in place, however, the success of this plan depends upon the strength of the board of directors and other key volunteers and supporters who can take an active role in fundraising. Therefore, this year Our Organization is making its first priority the recruitment of new board members. These individuals will be called upon to make a significant personal contribution to the organization and to bring new donors and foundation funders into the fold.

Individual donors and foundations will be inspired to support Our Organization's work if its programs are effective. For this reason, Our Organization's director will also dedicate significant time this year to standardizing and refining all of Our Organization's programs.

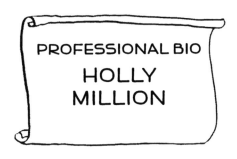

PROFESSIONAL BIO
HOLLY
MILLION

FOR fifteen years, Holly Million has been a professional fundraiser, serving nonprofit organizations and independent filmmakers in the San Francisco Bay Area. Experienced in meeting $1 million+ fundraising goals, Holly has worked for such nonprofit organizations as Interplast, SFJAZZ, KTEH Public Television, Goodwill, Amnesty International, Acterra, and GirlSource. In 1997, Holly secured funding for the Academy Award-winning film, *A Story of Healing*. A busy fundraising consultant, Holly travels around the country to lead workshops for nonprofit boards and staff on how to raise money from individual donors. She has a BA from Harvard and an MA from Stanford.